SHAUN RANKIN'S
SEASONED ISLANDS

To the lady that started me on my journey in life and in cooking. Unfortunately, she is not here to see it, but this is dedicated to the maker of the best corned beef and potato pie in the world.

To you Mum.

Love Shaun

AUTHOR'S NOTE

In the Channel Islands we are blessed with a wonderful array of natural ingredients; all of the absolute highest quality, all produced locally. These ingredients marry the best of traditional knowledge passed down through generations with cutting-edge technology.

That is the beauty of the Channel Islands. Generally speaking they have the balance right; the balance between tradition and modernity, work and play, family and community, and I love living here.

I have lived and worked in Jersey since 1993. I am proud to call it my home and I am evangelical about the stunning produce available on land and in the sea. I call Jersey my nine-mile garden and with good reason. The vast majority of ingredients that I use come from within that radius and that makes me proud. I cook and live that way because I am passionate about sustainability and traceability, but mostly I do it because it tastes so good.

I decided to write this book to introduce some of our world-class suppliers to a wider audience and suggest some ways in which, by using simple, easy recipes, you can make the flavours come alive. You will not find Michelin star cooking within these pages; this book contains many of the simpler dishes that I cook for my family, either at home or outdoors.

Shaun Rankin

A LITTLE
ABOUT ME

I was born in Ferryhill in the north-east of England. My earliest cooking memories are of helping my mum in the kitchen at home, helping to make Sunday lunch and learning her love of flavours and simple ingredients. She was a really great cook and I still use some of her recipes today; indeed, some of them are in this book.

From those early days I was hooked on cooking and there was never a doubt in my mind what I would do with my life. Three years at catering college from the age of 16 set me up for a decade of gaining experience in great restaurants across England, France, Australia and America, before I took a job in Jersey back in 1993. I have never moved away from the island since and never will. That is the effect Jersey can have on you and I know many, many people who have a similar tale to tell; travelled the globe; landed in Jersey for a short stop, but never wanted to leave.

I won my first Michelin star in 2004, just a year after opening a new restaurant – Bohemia. We were named in the top 20 restaurants in the *The Good Food Guide* 2009 and have successfully maintained our Michelin star. A fantastic accolade, but that aside, I genuinely cook for the love of it and the joy of creating good food, just as my mum taught me.

WELCOME
TO THE ISLANDS

The Channel Islands are made up of eight inhabited islands and several smaller ones, nestled in close to the coast of France but they are British Crown Dependencies.

A strong French influence is apparent everywhere, but the people are proud of their British allegiance, which they have pledged for more than 800 years. However, ask those that live here (roughly 90,000 in Jersey, 60,000 in Guernsey, down to just 600 in Herm) what their nationality is and they will tell you that they are Islanders; showing traits of independence, community and eccentricity mixed with a laid back attitude to life; something that characterises most who live surrounded by the sea the world over.

The islands are fortunate to sit within a body of sea that has a huge tidal flow, one of the fastest in the world, which supplies us with an abundance of spectacular seafood. The statistics show that we also generally get more annual sunshine than the mainland, making the climate better for those holidaying on our stunning golden-sand beaches as well as for the farmers growing their crops, such as the renowned Royal potato.

What's great about life here is that the pace of everything is just that bit more laid back, but not backward, I hasten to add! The islands are, in my view, real centres of excellence with top professionals and plenty of success stories. Probably the only real difference is that for us a big business commute is a 20 minute drive! The real plus is the work and life balance, which is still tipped towards life, and that for me holds huge value.

THE PRODUCERS

Over the years, I have built up relationships with people who, in my view, make the Channel Islands one of the greatest places in the world to live.

These people share my passion for producing food. I would like to introduce them and the Channel Islands to you. Throughout this book we have taken time to focus on some of these great characters in more depth, I hope you enjoy their stories as much as the recipes.

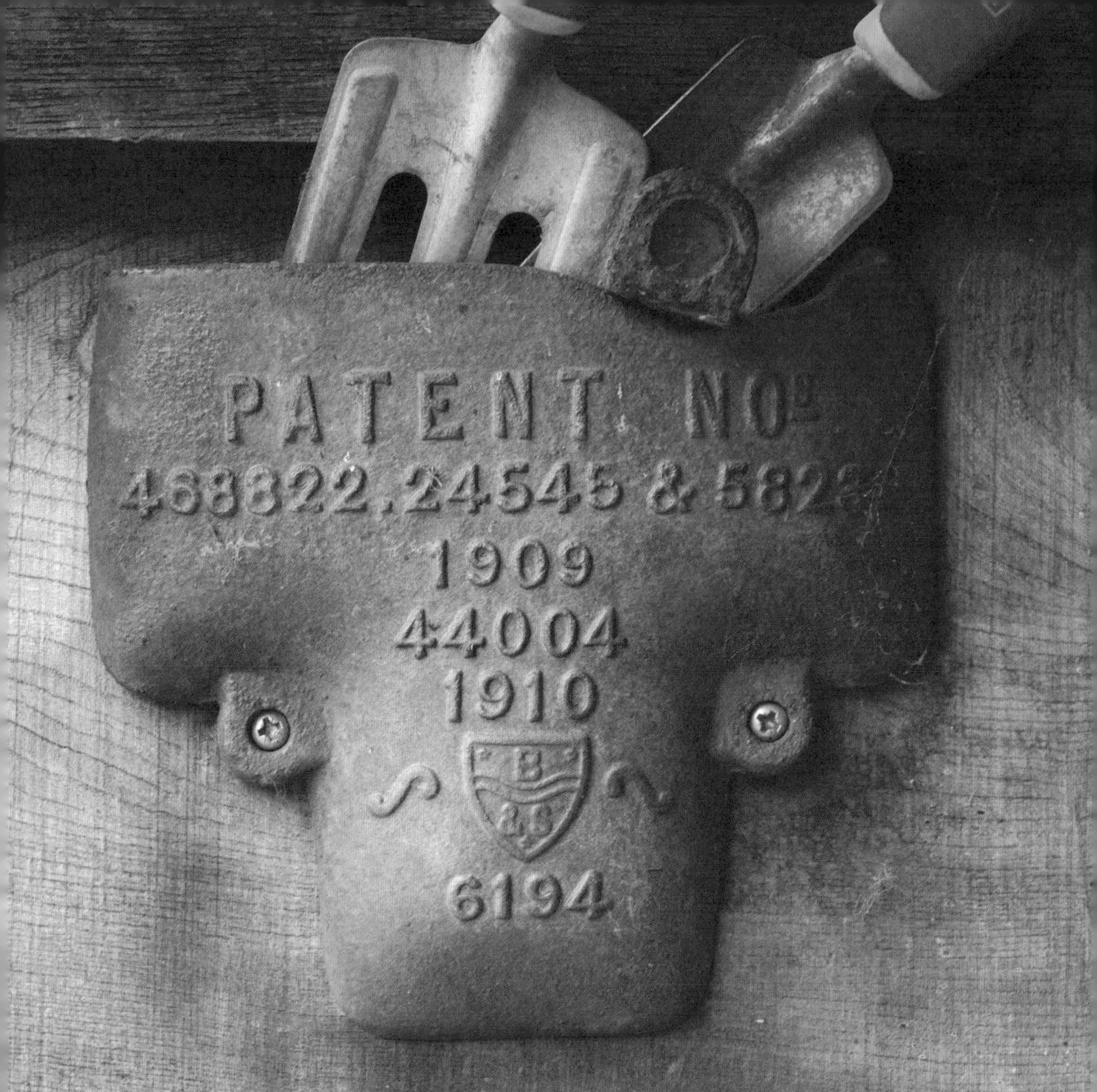

First published in 2010

The Refinery
11 Peter Street, St. Helier,
Jersey, JE2 4SP
www.getrefined.com

Produced in Jersey, Channel Islands
Printed in England by JW Marcom Ltd

Publisher: Chris Shelton
Editor: Natasha Egré
Recipes: Shaun Rankin
Photographer: Matt Porteous
Design Director: Ben Hickingbotham
Senior Designer: Paul Le Fondré

Copyright © 2010 by Shaun Rankin
www.shaunrankin.com

Photography, design and layout
© The Observatory
www.beobserved.com

A CIP catalogue record for this book is
available from the British Library.

ISBN 978-0-9566796-0-4

www.shaunrankin.com

CONTENTS

Breakfast & Brunch 10

Starters, Salads & Sides 28

Soups 56

Fish & Shellfish 76

Meat, Game & Poultry 108

Pasta & Vegetarian 144

Desserts 162

Breads 192

Pantry 202

Index 212

BREAKFAST & BRUNCH

JAMIE RACJAN FUNGI DELECTI

A true marriage of tradition and science make Fungi Delecti what it is today.

As a chef, I am always looking for something new to put in recipes, to make my menus more exciting, and the guys at Fungi Delecti never let me down

They produce a wide range of products; some traditionally and some using unique homemade contraptions.

Fungi Delecti was set up in 1996 after carrying out specialised growing trials in conjunction with Plymouth University, to see if shiitake mushrooms could be grown in Jersey using traditional Japanese methods. They could and still do on a considerable scale. Since then, they have progressed to growing oyster mushrooms and all sorts of weird and wonderful food.

This is a family run business with a passion for the islands. They have an understanding of the need to create a sustainable business, which contributes to the environment as much as it takes from it.

There are many unusual products harvested on the Fungi Delecti Farm, but perhaps the strangest are the mushrooms grown on specially drilled oak logs which act as incubators for two years while the fungi grow. This means the mushrooms are true to the original Japanese method, ensuring a superior texture and taste.

The beauty of these pancakes is that you can pre-cook them and then just flash them for 20 seconds in the microwave to reheat when you want to serve. Great for the large or busy family.

AMERICAN-STYLE PANCAKES WITH HONEY, GREEK YOGURT & PECAN NUTS

Serves 6

(Makes 12)

Special equipment

Crêpe pan

Ingredients

2 eggs

220g (8oz) caster sugar

180g (6oz) unsalted butter, melted

340g (12oz) plain flour, sifted

½ tsp baking powder

450ml (15fl oz) milk

1 tsp vanilla essence

To Serve

Pecan nuts

Honey

Plain yogurt

Honeycomb

1 Whisk the eggs and sugar together in a large mixing bowl.

2 Add the butter, flour, baking powder, milk and vanilla essence. Mix well, making sure there are no lumps.

3 Heat a dry crêpe pan and pour in half a ladle of batter, immediately tilting the pan with your other hand to spread the batter evenly.

4 Cook until the edges begin to colour and you see small bubbles appearing all over the surface, and then flip the pancake (you can use a fish slice if this is easier).

5 Cook for a few moments on the other side and then slide onto a plate. If you want to serve straight away, keep warm until all the pancakes are cooked.

6 To serve, top with pecan nuts, drizzle with honey and finish with a dollop of plain yogurt.

A great snack mid-morning. The muffins are at their best served slightly warm accompanied by a frothy cappuccino.

APPLE & CINNAMON MUFFINS

Makes 10–12

Special equipment

12 muffin cases

Ingredients

225g (8oz) plain flour

3 tsp baking powder

1 tsp salt

20g (¾oz) ground cinnamon

1 tsp ground nutmeg

1 tsp ground ginger

100g (3½oz) caster sugar

1 egg

150ml (5fl oz) milk

3 tbsp sunflower oil

40g (1½oz) unsalted butter, melted

170g (6oz) Granny Smith apples, cored, peeled and diced

70g (2½oz) golden sultanas

3 tbsp light soft brown sugar

1 Heat the oven to 190°C (375°F/Gas 5).

2 Place the muffin cases in a cake tray.

3 In a large bowl, sift together the flour, baking powder, salt, cinnamon, nutmeg, ginger and sugar.

4 In a separate bowl, beat the egg and stir in the milk. Add the oil, melted butter and stir in the diced apple.

5 Add the wet mixture into the dry and stir in well. Add the golden sultanas.

6 Spoon the mixture into the muffin cases and sprinkle the tops with brown sugar.

7 Bake in the oven for 20 minutes until lightly brown. They should spring back when pressed.

8 Allow to cool slightly before eating.

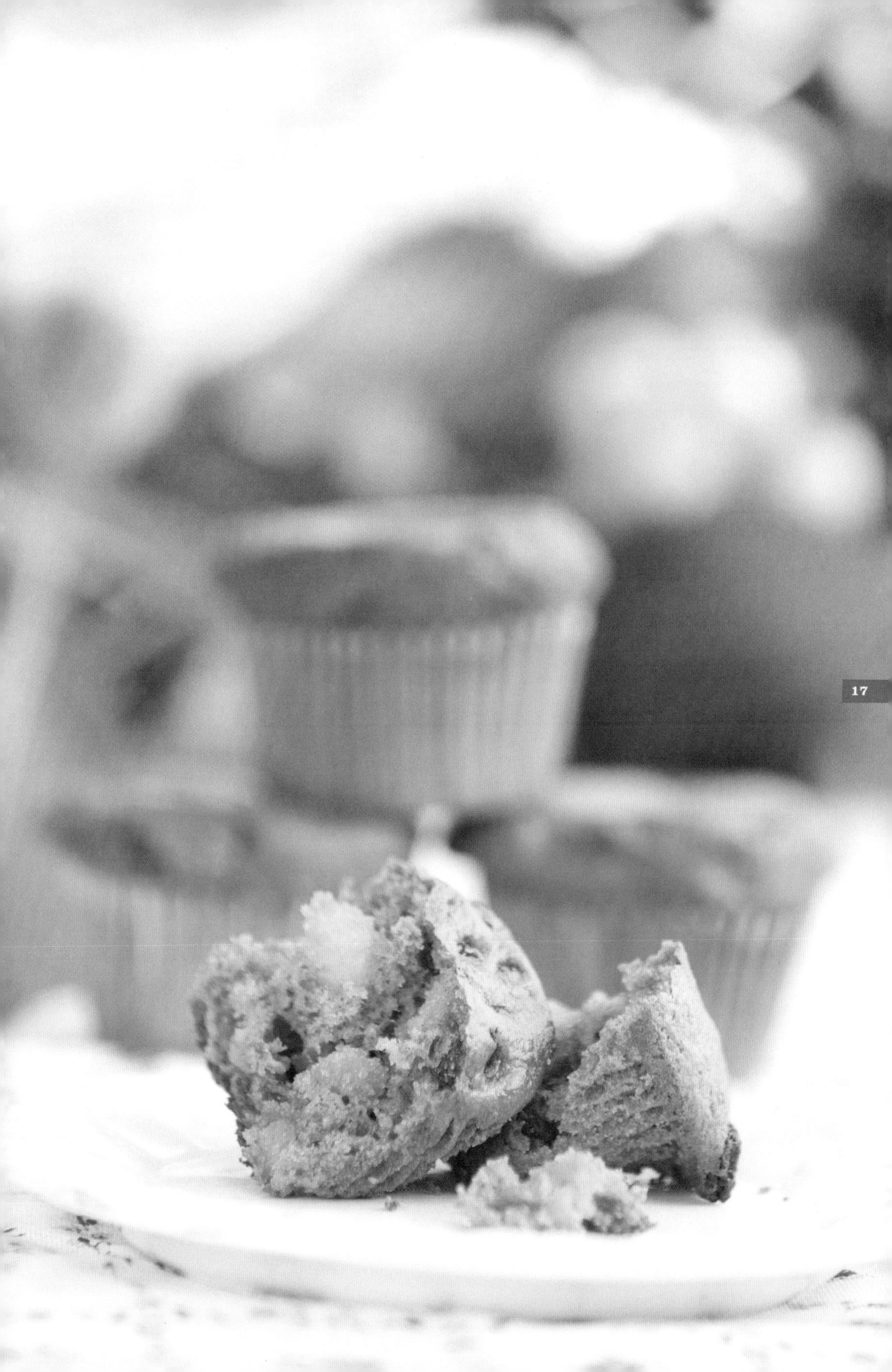

This is one of my favourite ways to kick start the weekend. The maple syrup and smoked bacon are really good together. Give it a try!

FRENCH TOAST WITH SMOKED BACON, MAPLE SYRUP & ROCKET SALAD

Serves 4

Ingredients

4 eggs

1 tbsp milk

Pinch of nutmeg

4 slices of white bread, thick cut

2 tsp vegetable oil

8 smoked back bacon rashers

50g (1¾oz) rocket salad

To Serve

Maple syrup

1 Crack the eggs into a large deep-sided bowl. Add the milk and nutmeg and whisk together by hand.

2 Dip the slices of bread into the mixture, ensuring that both sides are covered. The bread will soak up the egg mix but do not leave it in the mix for a prolonged period, as it will disintegrate.

3 Add 1 tsp of oil to a large frying pan over a high heat. Once warm, place the soaked bread slices in the pan (one at a time if need be) and cook on both sides until golden brown.

4 Meanwhile, heat 1 tsp of the vegetable oil in a separate frying pan over a high heat. Once warm, add the bacon and fry until crispy (alternatively, grill the bacon under a preheated grill).

5 Put the French toast onto plates immediately and arrange 2 rashers of crispy, smoked bacon on top of each slice. Add the rocket salad and, to finish, drizzle over the maple syrup to taste.

ROZEL BAY, JERSEY

No need for plates! Serve in the pan at the table with hot buttered toast.

GRILLED BLACK PUDDING WITH FRIED HEN'S EGGS, FORESTIERE GARNISH & WATERCRESS

Serves 2

Ingredients

100g (3½oz) black pudding

3½ tbsp olive oil

100g (3½oz) Jersey Royal potatoes, cooked and sliced

50g (1¾oz) shiitake mushrooms

4 eggs

20g (¾oz) unsalted butter

Sea salt and cracked black pepper

1 tsp chopped chives

Handful of watercress leaves

1 Preheat the grill to hot. Place the whole black pudding on a baking tray with ½ tbsp of the olive oil and grill for 3 minutes.

2 In a hot, non-stick frying pan, add 1 tbsp of the olive oil and fry the potato slices on both sides until golden brown and crispy. Remove the potatoes from the pan and keep warm.

3 Wipe the pan with some kitchen towel to remove the oil.

4 In the same pan add the remaining 2 tbsp of olive oil and the mushrooms and cook for 1 minute until tender.

5 Keeping the mushrooms in the pan, crack the eggs in and fry. When they are nearly cooked, add the butter to finish the eggs. Season with salt and pepper.

6 When the eggs are cooked, add the sautéed potatoes to the pan and place the black pudding in the centre. Sprinkle with the chopped chives and finish with the watercress leaves.

This dish is great any time of day but perfect as a treat for breakfast on Christmas Day.

WARM POTATO PANCAKE WITH SMOKED SALMON & SCRAMBLED EGGS

Serves 4

Special equipment

4 non-stick blini pans or similar moulds

Ingredients

2 tbsp sea salt

2 Marfona potatoes

12 eggs

1 tbsp chives

Salt and cracked black pepper

Olive oil

2 tbsp milk

20g (¾oz) unsalted butter

175g (6oz) smoked salmon

1 Preheat the oven to 160°C (325°F/Gas 3).

2 Sprinkle the sea salt on a small baking tray, place the potatoes on top and bake in the oven for 50 minutes.

3 When the potatoes come out, put the blini pans/moulds on a roasting tray and into the oven to get hot.

4 Cut the potatoes in half and scoop out the middle into a bowl. Discard the skins. Weigh out 250g (9oz) of potato and discard any excess. It is important at this stage that the potato is still warm.

5 Separate 4 of the eggs and add the yolks and half of the chives to the potato and whisk in well. Season with salt and black pepper.

6 In a clean bowl, whisk the egg whites to firm peaks.

7 Using a metal spoon, carefully fold the whisked egg whites into the potato mix, taking care not to knock the air out of the whites.

8 Lift the blini pans/moulds out of the oven and add a drizzle of olive oil to each.

9 Using a spoon, divide the potato mixture equally between the pans/moulds.

10 Put back into the oven and bake for 15 minutes until cooked and golden brown.

11 Allow to cool slightly before removing them from their pans/moulds. Keep warm.

12 Crack the remaining eggs into a bowl add the milk and whisk.

13 Heat the butter in a saucepan, add the egg mix and then turn the heat down to low.

14 Using a wooden spoon, move the egg mix in the pan until the eggs are just cooked. Finish with the remaining chives and remove from the heat.

15 To serve, place the pancakes in the middle of the plate, curl the smoked salmon on top and then add the creamy scrambled eggs.

The great thing about rarebit is that the mix will keep in the fridge for up to a week. So, you can have it for breakfast, lunch or even a snack at supper time. It's also great served with grilled black pudding and a cold beer!

WELSH RAREBIT WITH CURED BACON

Serves 2

Special equipment

Food processor

Ingredients

375ml (13fl oz) milk
125g (4½oz) unsalted butter
125g (4½oz) plain flour
1 tsp Worcestershire sauce
1 tbsp English mustard
4 tbsp beer
3 egg yolks
100g (3½oz) mature Cheddar, grated
Sea salt and cracked black pepper
2 pieces white bread, roughly cut, 2.5cm (1in) thick
4 smoked bacon rashers

1 Heat the milk in a saucepan over a medium heat. Keep warm.

2 Melt the butter in a separate saucepan. When completely melted, sift the flour into the butter and mix in well with a wooden spoon, taking care not to let it burn.

3 Stir the mix constantly until it is cooked through – this will be when you can no longer taste the flour.

4 Now start adding the warm milk, one ladle at a time, mixing well until it has all been absorbed. You will be left with a thick sauce.

5 Spoon the béchamel sauce into a bowl, cover with cling film and set aside in the fridge until cold and firm.

6 Add the Worcestershire sauce to the béchamel sauce with the mustard, beer and egg yolks and whisk until all the ingredients are thoroughly mixed in.

7 Preheat the grill to hot.

8 Stir in the cheese and season with salt and pepper to your liking.

9 Under the grill, toast the bread lightly on both sides.

10 Thickly spread the rarebit mixture onto the toast on one side.

11 Place the smoked bacon rashers under the hot grill for 2–3 minutes each side or until crispy. Remove and put aside.

12 Place the rarebit toasts under the grill for about 5 minutes or until the cheese is golden brown.

13 Remove from under the grill, top with the smoked bacon and serve straight away.

STARTERS
SALADS
& SIDES

WILLIAM CHURCH
THE JERSEY ROYAL COMPANY

There is an old Jersey tale that explains the origins of the Jersey Royal potato:

A farmer called Hugh De La Haye had a strange shaped potato with 15 eyes. De La Haye cut the potato into 15 parts and gave one shoot to 14 friends to see if it was possible to reproduce the potato. Only one of the shoots sprouted, but the potatoes it grew were small and deliciously sweet.

It was a fortuitous accident and explains why initially Jersey Royals were called the Jersey Royal Flukes.

These gems have been grown in Jersey for more than 130 years and remain the island's unique trademark. Jersey people know it's spring when, on brisk early mornings on the steep south-facing fields, workers appear digging up the potatoes by hand, as they have always done.

The Jersey Royal Company is one of Jersey's largest businesses, but has very humble origins. It started as a collection of local farmers and now employs more than 600 people and sells our finest asset in large quantities to the UK and further afield. The demand for Royals always outstrips production, as their fantastic flavour is valued far beyond our island boundaries.

This is my twist on a classic recipe. The warm mushrooms bring a new dimension to the dish and it's great with some toasted focaccia or olive bread (see pages 194 and 196).

CARPACCIO OF FILLET WITH A HORSERADISH BAVOIRE & WOODLAND MUSHROOM SALAD

Serves 4

Ingredients

500g (1lb 2oz) beef fillet
200ml (7fl oz) double cream
4 egg yolks
3 tbsp horseradish purée
Salt and cracked black pepper
1 tbsp mayonnaise (see page 206)
Juice of 1 lemon
3 tbsp double cream, whipped
250g (9oz) woodland mushrooms, sliced
15g (½oz) unsalted butter
50g (1¾oz) rocket and watercress salad
Olive oil
Parmesan cheese shavings, to serve

1 Preheat the oven to 125°C (260°F/Gas 1).

2 Roll the beef fillet tightly in cling film so it stays in a nice cylindrical shape and place in the fridge to firm up.

3 In a saucepan, bring the double cream to the boil. Place the egg yolks in a mixing bowl, then pour the cream over the yolks and whisk continuously.

4 Add 2 tbsp of the horseradish purée and whisk well. Season with salt and pepper.

5 Pour the mixture into an ovenproof terrine mould.

6 Place the terrine into a roasting tray with deep sides. Pour hot water into the roasting tray, making sure that the water only comes half way up the side of the terrine.

7 Carefully place in the oven and cook for about 35 minutes until set.

8 Once cooked, remove from the water bath, allow to cool, then place in the fridge until cold.

9 Whisk the remaining horseradish purée into the mayonnaise and add half the lemon juice.

10 Fold the whipped double cream into the mayonnaise mixture.

11 Remove the terrine from the fridge and in a bowl mix 5 parts of the horseradish bavoire to 1 part of the cream mixture. Store in a clean container in the fridge until needed.

12 Slice the beef fillet thinly with a sharp knife and arrange onto the plates (if you find it difficult to slice the beef thinly you can put the slices between 2 pieces of cling film and use a meat hammer to flatten out). Season with salt and pepper.

13 In a hot frying pan, cook the mushrooms in the butter, season and finish with the remaining lemon juice.

14 Arrange the hot woodland mushrooms and rocket and watercress salad over the beef. Drizzle with a little olive oil, add a dollop of horseradish bavoire and scatter over Parmesan cheese shavings.

If you don't have time to make your own brioche, you can get it now in many good supermarkets.

CHICKEN LIVER PARFAIT WITH APPLE & QUINCE PUREE & WARM TOASTED BRIOCHE

Serves 6

Special equipment

Blender

Ingredients

330g (11oz) chicken livers
250ml (8fl oz) milk
300ml (10fl oz) Madeira
300ml (10fl oz) port
300ml (10fl oz) white wine
2 sprigs of rosemary
2 sprigs of thyme
2 garlic cloves
2 tsp salt
1 large egg
125g (4½oz) unsalted butter
2 Granny Smith apples
2 quince
Juice of 1 lemon
50g (1¾oz) quince jam
Brioche (see page 204)

Preparation

1 Trim all sinew off the chicken livers and place the livers in a container. Submerge in the milk and cover with cling film. Leave to soak in the fridge overnight.

Method

1 Put the Madeira, port, wine, rosemary, thyme and garlic into a saucepan and bring to the boil. Reduce the liquid until you have 100ml (3½fl oz)left. Strain and keep the syrup warm.

2 Preheat the oven to 140°C (275°F/Gas 1).

3 Strain the livers from the milk and place in a food blender. Add the salt and egg.

4 Melt the butter in a saucepan, but do not allow it to boil. Keep warm.

5   Start to blend the livers on full speed. After 2 minutes, add the warm alcohol syrup and the hot melted butter. Blend for a further 2 minutes and then pass through a sieve into a bowl.

6   Fill the terrine mould with your mixture, making sure to tap it on a hard surface to remove any trapped air.

7   Place a lid on the terrine mould or cover with foil. Put in a deep baking tray and add warm water until half way up the sides of the mould. Place in the oven and cook for around 15 minutes until the parfait has a slight wobble.

8   Once cooked, remove from the tray, cool slightly and then chill in the fridge until needed.

9   For the apple and quince purée, peel, core and quarter the apples and quince. Cover with water and half the lemon juice to retain the colour.

10 Place the quince in a saucepan, add the juice of half a lemon, and heat for 5 minutes. Add the apples and cook for a further 10–15 minutes until both are soft.

11 Place in a blender with the jam and blend until smooth. Store in the fridge until needed.

12 To serve, dip the terrine into hot water for a moment to loosen the parfait and turn out onto a platter. Slice and serve with the apple and quince purée and toasted brioche.

Panko breadcrumbs are often used in Japanese cooking and have a crispier, airier texture. This is basically just posh eggs with soldiers!

CRISPY POACHED DUCK EGGS WITH GRIDDLED ASPARAGUS

Serves 4

Special equipment

Deep fat fryer

Ingredients

12 asparagus spears

1 tbsp white wine vinegar

4 duck eggs

Plain flour, for dusting

2 hen's eggs, beaten

150g (5½oz) Panko breadcrumbs

About 500ml (16fl oz) sunflower oil, for deep frying

1 tbsp olive oil

Sea salt and cracked black pepper

Celery salt, to taste

50g (1¾oz) rocket

1 Wash the asparagus and snap off the bottom of the stalks (about 2cm/1¾in). Place in a steamer and cook for 2 minutes. Put aside.

2 Bring a saucepan of water to the boil and add the white wine vinegar. Turn down the heat to medium and poach the duck eggs in the simmering vinegar water for 4 minutes then carefully spoon out into iced cold water to stop them cooking further.

3 Once cool, remove the eggs from the water and dry on a clean towel.

4 Dust the eggs with plain flour and carefully place into the beaten eggs, remove and carefully roll in the Panko breadcrumbs.

5 Preheat the deep fat fryer to 170°C (340°F). Alternatively, half fill a deep saucepan with the sunflower oil and, using a cooking thermometer, heat to 170°C (340°F).

6 Carefully place the eggs into the oil using a slotted spoon and fry for 2–3 minutes or until golden brown and crispy.

7 In a hot griddle pan, brown the asparagus spears in olive oil and season with salt and pepper.

8 To finish, place 1 egg on each plate, cut in half and season with celery salt. Divide the griddled asparagus spears between the plates and add some rocket salad.

The sweetness of the scallops works fantastically with the aromatic curry spices. I like to serve this with crispy onion bhajis on the side.

CURRIED SCALLOPS WITH COCONUT & CORIANDER DAHL & APPLE SALAD

Serves 4

Ingredients

For the dahl

150g (5½oz) red lentils

240ml (8fl oz) chicken stock (see page 207)

2 tsp turmeric

Salt

50g (1¾oz) unsalted butter

1 onion, peeled and diced

2 tsp cumin seeds

100ml (3½fl oz) coconut milk

50g (1¾oz) baby spinach

Small bunch of coriander, chopped

For the curried scallops

4 tsp curry powder

2 tsp salt

12 scallops, removed from their shells, cleaned and coral removed

Olive oil, for frying

To garnish

1 apple

1 tomato, skin removed

Preparation

1. Thoroughly rinse the red lentils under cold water and then soak overnight in cold water.

Method

1. To make the dahl, first strain the red lentils.

2. In a large saucepan, heat the chicken stock over a medium heat. Add the turmeric, season with salt and add the red lentils. Bring to the boil and then simmer for 15–20 minutes or until the lentils are tender. When ready, strain the lentils and discard the cooking juices.

3. Melt the butter in a pan and sauté the onion with the cumin seeds until browned.

4. Add the lentils, coconut milk, baby spinach and three quarters of the coriander and cook on a medium heat until heated through. Keep warm.

5. To cook the scallops, make the curry salt by mixing together in a bowl the curry powder and salt.

6. Dip the scallops one by one into the curry salt (one side only). Knock off the excess powder by tapping your wrist and place the scallops on a plate with the curry salt side facing up.

7. For the garnish, peel and remove the core of the apple then slice into 5mm (¼in) sticks. Dice the tomato.

8. Add some olive oil to a hot frying pan. Place the scallops, curry salt side down, in the pan. Cook the scallops for 1 minute each side, until golden brown.

9. Spoon the warm dahl onto 4 plates and arrange the scallops on top. Place the apple on top of the scallops and garnish with the remaining chopped coriander and the diced tomato.

Oysters are great any time of day. Here are three alternative dressings for you to try.

FRESH OYSTERS WITH THREE DRESSINGS
GIN & TONIC MINT JELLY, SHALLOT & RED WINE VINEGAR & CUCUMBER PICKLE

Serves 4

Special equipment

3 airtight jars

Ingredients

24 freshly shucked oysters, on ice

To serve

Crushed ice

1 lime, sliced

1 tsp caster sugar

10g sachet of gelatine, soaked in 2 tbsp cold water

3 tbsp gin

200ml (7fl oz) tonic water

1 lime, skinned and cut into small segments

Handful of mint, chopped

To serve, fill a shallow dish with crushed ice and place the oysters on top in their shells.

Fill little pots with the dressings and serve with some slices of fresh lime.

Gin & tonic mint jelly dressing

1 Heat 2 tsp of water in a pan. Add the caster sugar and dissolve. Add the gelatine.

2 Remove from the heat and cool slightly. Then add the gin and tonic.

3 Line a shallow (about 1cm/½in deep) flat tray with cling film. Pour the liquid on top.

4 Sprinkle over the lime segments and the chopped mint. Chill in the fridge until set.

5 Remove from the lined tray and cut into 1cm (½in) cubes. Store in an airtight jar.

Shallot & red wine vinegar dressing

80ml (2½fl oz) red wine vinegar
250ml (8fl oz) red wine, preferably Cabernet Sauvignon
125ml (4fl oz) ruby port
1 shallot, finely chopped

1 Reduce a generous 1 tbsp of the red wine vinegar to a syrup consistency in a saucepan over a high heat.

2 Add the red wine and port. Continue to reduce until sweet. Allow to cool.

3 Once cool, add the remaining red wine vinegar.

4 Add the shallot and pour into an airtight jar. This dressing will keep fresh for up to 6 months when refrigerated in an airtight container.

Cucumber pickle dressing

100g (3½oz) caster sugar
150ml (5fl oz) distilled rice vinegar
1 tbsp finely chopped cucumber
1 tsp finely chopped dill

1 Add the caster sugar, vinegar and 100ml (3½fl oz) of water to a pan.

2 Bring to the boil and dissolve the sugar.

3 Remove from the heat and allow to cool, then add the cucumber and dill. Stir and decant into an airtight jar.

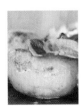

This makes a fantastic salad for a barbecue or a great potato dish for a Sunday roast.

ROAST JERSEY ROYAL SALAD WITH MAPLE SYRUP, GARLIC, RED ONION & CRISPY PANCETTA

Serves 4–6

Ingredients

4 tbsp olive oil

2 small red onions, peeled and quartered

4 sprigs of thyme

Salt and cracked black pepper

6 slices pancetta

900g (2lb) Jersey Royal potatoes, washed

1 garlic bulb, peeled and cut in half

3 tbsp maple syrup

1 Preheat the oven to 100°C (210°F/lowest Gas).

2 Heat a small frying pan, add 1 tbsp of the olive oil and brown the onions on their flat sides.

3 Remove the onions from the pan and place on foil on a baking tray. Add the oil from the pan and a sprig of thyme. Season with salt and pepper and wrap the foil over the onions. Place the tray in the oven and cook for 35 minutes or until tender.

4 While the onions cool, lay the pancetta strips on a baking tray with greaseproof paper and cook in the oven for 15–20 minutes, or until golden and crispy. Set aside until needed.

5 Break the cooled onions into petals.

6 Turn the oven up to 180°C (350°F/Gas 4) and heat up a clean roasting tray.

7 Put the Jersey Royals into a saucepan, cover with cold water and a good pinch of salt. Cook until you can pierce through with a small knife. This should take 6–8 minutes but will depend on the size of the Royals. Drain the potatoes well.

8 Remove the roasting tray from the oven and add the remaining 3 tbsp of olive oil. Carefully tip in the potatoes, add the garlic and 1 sprig of thyme and put back in the oven for 6 minutes, or until golden brown.

9 Remove from the oven and pour over the maple syrup, add the roasted red onion petals and mix all together. Place back in the oven for 2 minutes.

10 Remove from the oven and spoon the potatoes into a serving dish, break up the pancetta strips and sprinkle over the top and finish with a little more thyme.

This recipe is the perfect way to use up those leftover Jersey Royals in the fridge. It's so easy and quick to make – and delicious!

ROAST JERSEY ROYALS WITH GLAZED PEAR, ROQUEFORT CHEESE & WALNUT SALAD

Serves 4

Ingredients

400g (14oz) cooked Jersey Royal potatoes, cut into slices

3 tbsp olive oil

4 pears, peeled, cored and cut into quarters

20g (¾oz) caster sugar

2 tbsp Poire William

Knob of butter

60g (2oz) whole walnuts

100g (3½oz) Roquefort cheese

Bunch of watercress

1 In a large frying pan, sauté the Jersey Royals in 2 tbsp olive oil until golden brown. Remove the Royals from the pan and keep warm.

2 Re-using the same pan, add another 1 tbsp of olive oil and sauté the pears until they start to turn golden brown. Sprinkle with some caster sugar and allow to caramelise, moving the pears so the sugar does not burn. When golden, add the Poire William (take care as the pears may set alight).

3 Finish the pears with the butter. Remove from the heat and mix in the walnuts.

4 Arrange the warm Jersey Royals on plates with the glazed pears and walnuts. Crumble the Roquefort cheese over the top and serve with watercress salad. If desired, pour the leftover pan juices over the salad as a dressing.

SHAUN DIVING FOR SCALLOPS

This is a beautifully simple salad that also tastes great. If you want to enhance the dish, dress the French beans in truffle oil.

ROAST SCALLOPS WITH AVOCADO, FRENCH BEANS & HAZELNUT DRESSING

Serves 4

Special equipment

Glass jar with lid

Ingredients

2 tbsp hazelnut oil

3 tbsp olive oil, plus extra for frying

1 tsp wholegrain mustard

1 tsp white wine vinegar

12 large scallops

45g (1½oz) cooked French beans

2 avocados, sliced

Salt and cracked black pepper

20g (¾oz) unsalted butter

45g (1½oz) roasted hazelnuts

Juice of ½ lemon

85g (3oz) lamb's lettuce

1 To make the dressing, place the hazelnut oil, olive oil, mustard and vinegar into a glass jar, screw the lid on tight and shake well to emulsify. Leave aside until needed.

2 Wash the scallops in cold water and blot dry on kitchen paper.

3 Split the French beans in half lengthways and place in a bowl. Add the sliced avocados and enough vinaigrette to dress. Season with salt and pepper.

4 Heat some olive oil in a non-stick frying pan and fry the scallops for 1 minute on each side until golden.

5 Add the butter and roasted hazelnuts to the pan and warm through. Finish with the lemon juice and remove from the heat.

6 Divide the French bean and avocado salad between 4 serving plates and top with the scallops. Scatter the lamb's lettuce on and around the scallops. Drizzle the warm hazelnut pan juices over each plate.

Makes a great starter for a dinner party as you can prepare it in the morning and just serve when you're ready.

SMOKED SALMON TERRINE WITH CUCUMBER & SOFT QUAIL'S EGGS

Serves 4

Special equipment

Food processor

Ingredients

125g (4½oz) unsalted butter

400g (14oz) smoked salmon

125g (4½oz) whipping cream

Crushed pink peppercorns

1 cucumber

4 quail's eggs

Sunflower seed bread (see page 200), to serve

Preparation

1 To make clarified butter, melt the butter completely in a saucepan.

2 The butter will separate and there will be a milky residue on top. Using a spoon, carefully remove and discard the residue.

3 Underneath you should find golden liquid butter. Pour this off slowly into another pan leaving the milky water behind.

Method

1 Weigh out 150g (5½oz) smoked salmon. Lay the slices across the inside of a terrine mould, making sure they overlap and are long enough to reach up the sides of the terrine and cover the top when filled.

2 Place the remaining smoked salmon in a food processor and blend until smooth.

3 In separate pans, warm the clarified butter and the cream.

4 Slowly add the cream and then the clarified butter to the blended smoked salmon and blend until smooth.

5 Season with crushed pink peppercorns. Pour the mixture into the terrine mould.

6 Fold over the overhanging salmon slices to cover the top. Cover the whole terrine with cling film and place in the refrigerator to chill for at least 4 hours, preferably 6–8 hours, before slicing and serving.

7 Just before serving, peel the cucumber and then, using the peeler, create cucumber ribbons. Set aside.

8 Bring a saucepan of water to the boil. Carefully add the quail's eggs and cook for 2 minutes 45 seconds. Remove from the saucepan and rinse in cold water. Peel, slice in half and place on serving plates.

9 Add a slice of terrine to each plate and accompany with a swirl of cucumber ribbons and chunks of bread.

This is such a simple starter that is great for serving up at dinner parties. It's not labour intensive but will still impress your guests with its fabulous flavours.

SWEET CHILLI CHICKEN WITH GARLIC, LEMON & CORIANDER

Serves 2

Ingredients

2 chicken breasts, skinned

2 tbsp olive oil

½ tsp peeled and grated ginger

1 tbsp sweet chilli sauce

3 garlic cloves, peeled and finely chopped

Grated zest of 1 lemon

Grated zest of 1 lime

Sea salt and cracked black pepper

1 tbsp chopped coriander

6 pak choi leaves

50g (1¾oz) baby herb salad

Preparation

1 Cut the chicken breasts into strips and place in a large bowl.

2 Add the olive oil, ginger, sweet chilli sauce, garlic, lemon and lime zest. Season with a good pinch of salt and pepper and finally add the chopped coriander. Mix well and leave in the fridge to marinate for 1 hour.

Method

1 Heat a wok over a high heat.

2 Add the chicken pieces by hand. Don't stir them around the wok at this stage as they need to caramelise straight away.

3 Once the pieces are golden brown on one side, turn the strips and cook on the reverse until golden brown and cooked through.

4 Add the pak choi leaves just before you are ready to serve and stir in well.

5 Remove from the heat and divide between 2 plates. Garnish with a baby herb salad and spoon over the pan juices.

It's really important to source the best quality fresh tuna possible. The Bloody Mary Jelly works really well with the raw tuna and adds a bit of spice.

YELLOW FIN TUNA WITH LIME & WHITE RADISH DRESSING & BLOODY MARY JELLY

Serves 4

Ingredients

3 gelatine leaves
250ml (8fl oz) tomato juice
3 tbsp vodka
½ tsp Worcestershire sauce
½ tsp Tabasco sauce
1 ripe avocado
1 tbsp crème fraîche
Juice of ½ lemon
Sea salt and cracked black pepper
1 lime
200g (7oz) Yellow Fin tuna, diced
1 tbsp olive oil
1 tsp chopped coriander
1 tsp chopped dill
4 scallops, sliced
White radish, sliced
Pea shoots, to garnish

1 To make the Bloody Mary jelly, put the gelatine leaves into cold water to soak.

2 Place the tomato juice, vodka, Worcestershire and Tabasco sauces in a pan and warm.

3 Add the gelatine to the Bloody Mary mix and whisk in well. Pour into a clean container and place in the fridge to set.

4 Peel the avocado and remove the stone. Place in a food processor along with the crème fraîche, lemon juice, salt and pepper and blend until smooth.

5 Grate the lime zest over the tuna and season with salt and pepper.

6 Juice the lime and mix with the olive oil and chopped herbs. Pour the marinade over the sliced scallops and white radish and season with salt and pepper. Leave to marinate for 3 minutes.

7 Arrange the diced tuna on the plates. Remove the Bloody Mary jelly from the fridge, cut into small cubes and arrange next to the tuna. Finally, add the scallops and white radish and spoon over the lime marinade. Garnish with fresh pea shoots.

SOUPS

COLIN ROCHE
JERSEY
WATERCRESS

In 1976 Colin Roche came to Jersey for a weekend break with some friends from Liverpool and fell in love with the island. He phoned his mother the following day and told her he was staying because he'd found paradise.

I can empathise because that's the same effect Jersey had on me when I first arrived.

Colin started to grow watercress to take advantage of the naturally moist marshland in the parish of St Martin; perfect conditions for growing the leaves. After finding the ideal location, he went to the pub and, like so many local agreements, sealed a land deal with a dairy farmer over a pint of local brew.

Colin grows 'Nasturtium Officinal', a French variety of watercress, which has a better flavour than the English variety. He says it's an art to grow watercress well and it can be incredibly hard work but, even after 30 years, he still enjoys it.

Can you remember when your mum cooked roast chicken and you stole the crispy skin? Well, this will certainly bring back all those fond memories.

CHICKEN & POTATO SOUP WITH SCALLOPS, CHORIZO & CHICKEN SCRATCHING

Serves 4

Special equipment

Liquidiser

Ingredients

1 raw chicken skin, from the breasts

250g (9oz) Marfona potatoes

1 tbsp olive oil

2 shallots, peeled and sliced

2 garlic cloves, peeled

400ml (14fl oz) chicken stock (see page 207)

3 tbsp milk

Salt and cracked black pepper

3 sprigs of thyme

For the garnish

50g (1¾oz) chorizo sausage

2 tbsp olive oil

4 scallops

20g (¾oz) unsalted butter

Juice of ¼ lemon

Handful of baby spinach

2 sprigs of thyme

1 Preheat the oven to 160°C (325°F/Gas 3).

2 Place the raw chicken skin between 2 pieces of greaseproof paper, lay on a baking tray and then top with another baking tray of the same size. Cook for 30 minutes until golden brown and crispy then remove from the oven and leave to cool.

3 Peel the potatoes and dice into 2.5cm (1in) pieces. Cover with cold water and put aside until needed.

4 Heat the olive oil in a saucepan. Add the shallots and 1 garlic clove and cook on a low heat, without colouring the ingredients, until soft.

5 Add the diced potato, 400ml (14fl oz) of water and the chicken stock to the saucepan. Bring to the boil, reduce the heat and simmer for about 20 minutes or until the potatoes are cooked and falling apart.

6 Add the milk and blend in a liquidiser until smooth. Season with salt and pepper to taste.

7 Pour the soup into a clean bowl and add the remaining garlic clove and 3 sprigs of thyme. Leave to cool to allow the flavours to infuse.

8 For the garnish, peel the skin off the chorizo sausage. Place in a frying pan with 1 tbsp of the olive oil and warm through slowly until golden brown on the outside. Slice the chorizo and keep warm in the pan until needed. The oil will turn a deep ruby red; keep it for finishing the soup.

9 Cut the scallops in half into discs and season with salt and pepper. In a hot pan, add 1 tbsp of the olive oil and cook the scallops for 1 minute on each side until golden. Finish by adding the butter and lemon juice.

10 Remove the garlic and thyme from the soup and reheat.

11 To serve, pour the soup into bowls, sprinkle with the baby spinach, pan-fried scallops, sliced chorizo sausage and pieces of the crispy chicken skin. Drizzle a little of the chorizo oil over the top and add some thyme leaves.

For me, Colin Roche in Jersey grows the best watercress in the world. In this recipe, the deep peppery flavour of his watercress contrasts with the fresh crunchy pear.

CHILLED WATERCRESS SOUP WITH DRESSED ASIAN PEAR & GARDEN PEAS

Serves 4

Special equipment

Food processor

Ingredients

150g (5½oz) unsalted butter

2 small onions, peeled and finely sliced

6 bunches of watercress, stalks removed

200ml (7fl oz) milk

Salt and cracked black pepper

1 Asian pear (or prickly pear)

Juice of ½ lemon

1 tsp caster sugar

4 tbsp cooked garden peas

1 Melt the butter in a large pan over a medium heat.

2 Add the onions and sauté until translucent.

3 Add the watercress (reserving some leaves for garnish), the milk and approximately 700ml (1¼ pints) of water to the pan and bring to the boil.

4 Once boiled, remove from the heat.

5 Ladle the mixture from the saucepan into a food processor and liquidise until smooth. Season with salt and pepper.

6 Peel the pear, take out the core and cut into fine strips. In a bowl, mix the pear strips with the lemon juice and sugar.

7 Serve the soup either hot or cold, and garnish with the peas, dressed Asian pear and a few watercress leaves.

I use chicken stock for my French onion soup mainly because I think it works really well with the fresh thyme and Beaufort cheese. If you cannot get hold of Beaufort cheese, then Emmental will do just as well.

FRENCH ONION SOUP WITH THYME & BEAUFORT CHEESE CROUTES

Serves 4

Ingredients

6 tbsp olive oil
4 onions, peeled and finely sliced
Handful of thyme
50g (1¾oz) unsalted butter
100ml (3½fl oz) brandy
1 litre (1¾ pints) chicken stock (see page 207)
Sea salt and cracked black pepper
4 slices of olive bread (see page 196)
50g (1¾oz) Beaufort cheese, grated

1 Heat 2 tbsp of the olive oil in a large saucepan over a medium heat.

2 Add the onions, 2 sprigs of thyme and the butter and cook over a medium heat for 20 minutes, or until golden brown.

3 Add the brandy and reduce on a medium heat until the alcohol has evaporated.

4 Preheat the grill to hot.

5 Add the chicken stock to the onions and most of the remaining thyme (leave some to sprinkle on the croutons and the finished soup). Bring to the boil and then simmer for 20 minutes. Season with salt and pepper.

6 Meanwhile, for the giant croutes, dip the olive bread in 4 tbsp olive oil, making sure they are well covered. Then place the slices on a baking tray and cook under the grill for 10 minutes, or until golden brown and crispy.

7 To finish the croutes, sprinkle them with the Beaufort cheese, followed by some finely chopped fresh thyme and some salt to season.

8 Grill for a further 2 minutes, or until the cheese has melted.

9 To serve, ladle the soup into bowls and garnish with more thyme and a healthy serving of the warm baked olive bread croutes.

67

ST OUEN, JERSEY

This is a great refreshing soup for a hot summer's day. If you can't get sardines, mackerel will also work well.

GAZPACHO SOUP WITH GRILLED SARDINES ON TOAST

Serves 4

Special equipment

Food processor

Ingredients

1 red pepper, de-seeded and cut into quarters

750g (1lb 10oz) plum tomatoes, diced

2 red onions, peeled and chopped

1 cucumber, peeled, de-seeded and chopped

2 garlic cloves, peeled and chopped

Handful of coriander, chopped

½ red chilli, de-seeded and finely chopped

1½ tbsp passata

75ml (2½fl oz) olive oil, plus extra for drizzling

2½ tbsp red wine vinegar, preferably Cabernet Sauvignon

Sea salt and cracked black pepper

8 sardine fillets

Juice of ½ lemon

4 slices of sun-dried tomato bread (see page 198)

8 Parmesan cheese slices

Rocket, to serve

Preparation

1 Preheat the grill to hot. Grill the red pepper pieces on a baking sheet until blistered. Put them into a plastic bag and leave to cool, then peel.

2 Combine the peeled red pepper and all the other chopped vegetables with the garlic and coriander in a large bowl.

3 Add the chilli, passata, olive oil and vinegar and season with salt and pepper.

4 Mix together all the ingredients with your hands. Cover the bowl with cling film and place in the fridge. Leave to marinate overnight.

5 Place 4 glasses, suitable for serving the gazpacho, in the fridge for a few hours before serving.

Method

1. Remove the bowl of marinated vegetables and herbs from the fridge and pour half the mixture into a food processor. On the lowest speed setting, blend for 20 minutes. Set the liquid aside and repeat the process with the second batch.

2. Preheat the grill to hot.

3. Spoon the mixture through a fine sieve into a large bowl. Using the spoon, press down on the mixture to allow the gazpacho to run through the sieve. Repeat the process until all of the mixture has been passed through. Once finished, discard the leftover pulp. Check the seasoning, adding more salt and pepper if required. Then place in the fridge to chill until ready to serve.

4. Place the sardine fillets, skin side up, on a grill tray. Using your fingers, spread olive oil over the fillets. Pour over the lemon juice and season with salt and pepper to taste.

5. Place the sardines under the grill and cook for about 3 minutes, or until golden brown. Remove from the grill and keep warm.

6. Meanwhile, place the sun-dried tomato bread on a baking tray and grill on both sides. Lay 2 slices of Parmesan cheese on top of each toast and put back under the grill until the cheese has slightly melted, then remove.

7. To serve, remove the gazpacho soup and the chilled glasses from the fridge. Pour the cold soup into the glasses and drizzle a little olive oil over the top. Place the toast on serving plates, add some rocket and lay the sardine fillets on top. Serve straight away.

I like to use courgette flowers for this minestrone soup as they are in abundance in the summer months. Using a good quality pancetta is paramount when making this classic dish.

MINESTRONE SOUP WITH BABY COURGETTES

Serves 4

Ingredients

3 tbsp olive oil
1 onion, peeled and finely diced
½ leek, trimmed and finely chopped
1 celery stick, finely diced
2 garlic cloves, peeled and finely chopped
125g (4¼oz) pancetta, cut into strips
1 bay leaf
1 sprig of thyme
1 tsp tomato purée
100ml (3½fl oz) white wine
300ml (10fl oz) passata
1 litre (1¾ pints) chicken stock (see page 207)
85g (3oz) dried macaroni
4 baby courgettes, finely sliced (reserve courgette flowers for garnish)
4 tbsp garden peas
Sea salt and cracked black pepper
6 basil leaves
20g (¾oz) Parmesan cheese, finely grated

1 Heat the olive oil in a large saucepan over a medium heat. Add the onion, leek and celery and sauté until soft. Add the garlic, pancetta, bay leaf and thyme. Again, cook until soft.

2 Add the tomato purée to the pan, stir in and cook for a further 2 minutes. Then pour in the white wine, passata and chicken stock. Bring to the boil.

3 Add the macaroni, reduce the heat and simmer for about 15 minutes or until the pasta is nearly cooked.

4 Add the courgettes and peas to the pasta and continue to cook for a further 5 minutes, or until the macaroni and vegetables are cooked to your liking. Season with sea salt and pepper.

5 To serve, ladle the soup into bowls, top with courgette flowers, basil leaves and the Parmesan cheese.

I remember my mum would make this on cold winter days when I came in from school; it was the best thing ever!

MY MUM'S HAM HOCK, SPLIT YELLOW PEA & BARLEY SOUP

Serves 4

Ingredients

1 ham hock
1 carrot, peeled
1 onion, peeled and cut in half
2 garlic cloves, peeled
1 bay leaf
1 sprig of thyme
150g (5½oz) pearl barley
200g (7oz) yellow split peas
150g (5½oz) red lentils
Cracked black pepper
1 tbsp chopped flat-leaf parsley

Preparation

1 Place the ham hock in a large saucepan and cover with cold water. Leave to soak for 1 hour.

Method

1 Drain the soaked ham hock and cover once more with cold water.

2 Add the carrot, onion, garlic, bay leaf and thyme to the saucepan.

3 Bring to the boil then reduce the heat and simmer for 2 hours. After it has been cooking for 2 hours, remove the carrot and onion from the saucepan and continue to simmer.

4 Add the pearl barley and yellow split peas to the saucepan and cook for 50 minutes, then add the red lentils and cook for a further 10 minutes.

5 The whole cooking time should take no longer than 3 hours. The ham should fall off the bone when checked. Give it a further 15 minutes if needed.

6 Once cooked, carefully remove the ham hock from the saucepan with a large spoon, set aside on a plate and allow to cool just enough so you can remove the meat from the bone, it should just fall away easily.

7 Tear the meat into chunks – at this stage it's entirely up to you what size you want to keep the ham pieces. Return the ham back to the saucepan to warm through. Season with pepper and taste before adding any salt.

8 Ladle into soup bowls and finish with some chopped fresh parsley. Serve hot straight away with some crusty bread.

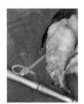

Serve chilled in the summer months for a lovely light lunch. Alternatively, you can serve it hot on winter days.

SWEETCORN & BASIL SOUP WITH CRISPY TEMPURA CRAB CLAWS

Serves 6–8

Special equipment

Food processor

Deep fat fryer

Ingredients

4 cobs of fresh corn

250g (9oz) unsalted butter

2 onions, peeled and finely sliced

Large handful of basil leaves

About 500ml (16fl oz) sunflower oil, for deep frying

Tempura batter (see page 208)

4 chancre crab claws, cooked and shells removed

Basil pesto, to serve

1 To make the corn stock, take a sharp knife and, holding the corn in an upright position, remove the kernels and place them in a bowl.

2 Place the cobs in a large saucepan and cover with water. Bring to the boil and simmer for approximately 15 minutes, or until the water takes on the flavour of the corn. Remove the cobs and reserve the liquid.

3 Melt the butter in a saucepan over a medium heat and then sauté the onions until soft and translucent.

4 Add the corn kernels and the sweetcorn stock and bring to the boil. Simmer until the corn has cooked through.

5 Ladle the corn liquid into a food processor and blend until smooth. To ensure a thin consistency, you may need to add a little water.

6 Pour the soup into a mixing bowl and add most of the basil leaves (leaving some for garnish).

7 After about 20 minutes strain the soup into a clean bowl and discard the basil leaves. Cover the soup with cling film and chill in the fridge until ready for serving.

8 Preheat the deep fat fryer to 180°C (350°F). Alternatively, half fill a deep saucepan with the sunflower oil and, using a cooking thermometer, heat to 180°C (350°F).

9 Dip the crab claws into the tempura batter so they are totally covered in the mixture and fry the claws in the deep fat fryer for 2 minutes, turning once, until golden brown.

10 To serve, ladle the soup into bowls and garnish with basil leaves, basil pesto and the hot, crispy crab claws on the side.

FISH & SHELLFISH

LOUIS JACKSON
THE FRESH FISH COMPANY

Louis Jackson started out by selling scallop meat to local restaurants. Over the years, his business has expanded into an operation that supplies restaurants across the Channel Islands and England as well.

The seafood in the Channel Islands is unsurpassed. I have eaten all over the globe at many of the finest restaurants but they cannot compete with the fresh produce found here, which literally goes from sea to serving in a matter of hours.

Not many places in the UK have this option, but here we almost take it for granted. We all know that seafood tastes best when it's fresh, and it doesn't get much fresher than when it is delivered straight from the fishermen's trawlers to the local restaurants, or to Vicky's thriving stall on Victoria Pier. This is undoubtedly a social hub for the island's discerning seafood lovers (and that's most of us!).

Louis' business is family-owned and run. They focus on only the finest catch, ethically fished and sensibly managed.

As a child my mother would take us to Whitby and we'd sit on the pier and eat fresh cockles off toothpicks. I couldn't write a recipe book without including a recipe for them.

COCKLES COOKED IN WHITE WINE WITH SHALLOTS, PANCETTA & BASIL

Serves 2

Ingredients

900g (2lb) cockles

4 slices of chorizo & Parmesan focaccia (see page 194)

2 tbsp olive oil

1 shallot, trimmed and sliced

1 garlic clove, peeled and sliced

90g (3oz) pancetta, diced into lardons

2 sprigs of thyme

300ml (10fl oz) white wine

6 basil leaves, roughly chopped

Cracked black pepper

1 Thoroughly rinse the cockles before cooking, discarding any that are broken. Scrub well to remove any sand, mud or grit. If shells are open, give them a light tap; if they do not close, discard.

2 Slice the chorizo bread and fry in a pan with olive oil until golden brown.

3 In a separate pan, sauté the shallot and garlic over a medium heat for about 2 minutes until the shallots are soft and translucent, but not coloured. Add the pancetta lardons followed by the cockles, thyme and finally the white wine. Steam with the lid on for 4 minutes, or until the shells have fully opened.

4 Spoon the cockles into a serving dish and sprinkle the basil leaves over them.

5 Pour over the cooking juices and finish with black pepper.

6 Serve with the toasted chorizo bread.

Whiting is a fish that is very much underrated. It has a great flavour, yet you rarely see it on restaurant menus. This dish is really simple to make and delicious to snack on. If you can't get hold of whiting fillets, then pollock or cod make good replacements.

CRISPY WHITING FINGERS IN LEMONADE BATTER WITH MINTED PEAS

Serves 2

Special equipment

Deep fat fryer

Ingredients

About 500ml (16fl oz) sunflower oil, for deep frying

320g (11oz) whiting fillet, skinned and cleaned

200ml (7fl oz) lemonade

110g (4oz) plain flour

250g (9oz) fresh or frozen peas

Sea salt and cracked black pepper

1 tsp white wine vinegar

8 mint leaves, roughly chopped

1 lime, quartered

2 tbsp tartare sauce (see page 205)

1 Preheat the deep fat fryer to 180°C (350°F). Alternatively, half fill a deep saucepan with the sunflower oil and, using a cooking thermometer, heat to 180°C (350°F).

2 Cut the whiting fillets so that you have 8 individual goujons. Set aside.

3 In a large mixing bowl, whisk together the lemonade and flour to make the batter. Set aside.

4 Add the peas to a saucepan, cover with water and bring to the boil. Cook for about 5 minutes, or until the peas are cooked but still nice and green.

5 Remove from the heat and drain, reserving the liquid. Measure out 180g (6oz) of the cooked peas and put into a food processor. Blend with 2 tbsp of the cooking liquid until you have a smooth purée. Discard the rest of the cooking liquid.

6 Add the remaining whole peas to the purée but do not blend. Season with salt and pepper, pour in the white wine vinegar and stir in the chopped mint. Cover with cling film and set aside, keeping warm until ready to serve.

7 Individually dip the whiting goujons in the bowl of lemonade batter so that they are totally covered. Carefully lower the fish into the deep fat fryer or saucepan and cook for 4 minutes, or until golden brown and crispy.

8 Remove from the fryer with a slotted spoon and set aside to drain on kitchen paper. Season to taste with salt.

9 Serve straight away with the minted peas, lime segments and spoonfuls of homemade tartare sauce.

The Asian flavours in this recipe bring a modern twist to traditional dressed crab.

DRESSED CRAB WITH SPRING ONIONS, TOASTED SWEETCORN, RED CHILLI & CORIANDER

Serves 2

Ingredients

2 live crabs
1 pinch of sea salt
1 tbsp of cooked basmati rice
Juice of 1 lime
1 red chilli, de-seeded and finely chopped
Salt and cracked black pepper
2 tbsp crème fraîche
2 spring onions, trimmed and finely chopped
1 tsp chopped coriander
2 baby pak choi

To garnish

1 tbsp sweetcorn kernels, cooked and toasted
1 tbsp chopped coriander
½ tsp chopped red chilli
1 tsp light soy sauce
¼ tsp peeled and grated fresh ginger

Preparation

1 If using live crabs, place them in a large pan and cover with cold water. Add salt and bring to the boil. Boil for 1 minute then remove from the water and place on a chopping board. Allow to cool.

2 When cool enough to handle, you can prepare the crabs. First remove the legs by twisting them off where they meet the body.

3 Remove the claws by pulling them away from the body.

4 Separate the body from the central part of the crab by placing the crab on its back. Put your hands under the edge of the crab and push upwards until you hear it break. You may need to use a heavy knife to help you lever the crab apart.

5 Remove all ten of the 'dead man's fingers' and discard.

6 Drain any excess water from the shell of the crab and remove the stomach sack and hard membranes inside the shell. Use a spoon to remove the brown meat from the shell and any soft shell that has formed. Place it into a clean bowl.

Method

7 Press down on the edges of the crab shell, breaking away the outer edges to form a 'dish' for serving.

8 Break each claw in half. Use the handle of a teaspoon to scrape the white meat out of the thick end of the claw. Place into a separate clean bowl.

9 Use the back of a heavy-bladed knife to crack open the remaining piece of claw and the pincers. Remove all the white meat and flake into the bowl. Remove the piece of cartilage inside each of the claws, pick off the meat and discard the cartilage.

10 To remove the meat from the body of the crab, take a sharp knife and cut the crab body in half, then in half again. Pick out the meat using your fingers.

11 If the legs are large enough, it's worth picking the meat out of them. Snap them in half and discard the thin end of the leg. Using the back of a heavy-bladed knife, smash the shell on the thicker part of the leg. Pull the meat out and add to your bowl.

1 Run your fingers through the white meat in the bowl to break up the meat and to pick out any remaining bits of shell.

2 Mix the brown meat with the cooked rice. Add the lime juice and the red chilli and season with salt and pepper.

3 To the bowl of white crab meat, add the crème fraîche, half of the spring onion and the coriander and seasoning. Use a fork to mix.

4 Refrigerate the crab mixtures while you thoroughly clean the crab shell.

5 Steam the baby pak choi for 2 minutes.

6 Spoon the brown crab meat into both sides of the cleaned crab shell. Then spoon the white crab mix into the centre of the shell.

7 Garnish with the sweetcorn, coriander, chilli and the remaining spring onions.

8 To serve, sit the steamed pak choi next to the dressed crab. Drizzle with soy sauce and sprinkle the grated ginger on top.

21 Serve with crusty bread.

Dover sole is one of my favourite fish to use as it can stand up to some strong flavours. In this recipe it works really well with the cured pancetta and garden peas.

GRILLED DOVER SOLE WITH GARDEN PEAS & CRISPY PANCETTA SALAD

Serves 2

Ingredients

6 slices of pancetta

1 whole Dover sole, on the bone with skin and skirts removed

Salt and cracked black pepper

50g (1¾oz) unsalted butter, cubed

1 shallot, peeled and finely chopped

1 bay leaf

360ml (12fl oz) white wine

150ml (5fl oz) double cream

50g (1¾oz) cooked garden peas

½ lemon

Bunch of watercress

2 tsp chopped chives

1 Preheat the oven to 150°C (300°F/Gas 2) and preheat the grill to hot.

2 Place the pancetta on a baking tray and bake in the oven for 15–20 minutes, or until brown and crispy. Leave to cool and then cut into small pieces.

3 Season the Dover sole on both sides with salt and pepper before placing it in a well-greased ovenproof dish. Top with the cubes of butter and grill for 4–5 minutes on each side, according to the thickness of the fish. Take care when turning the sole. Spread more butter over the top to stop it from drying out, if required. The fish should be white and slightly flaky, but still very tender.

4 Meanwhile, in a saucepan, mix together the chopped shallot, bay leaf and white wine. Bring to the boil and reduce the wine by half. Next add the cream and bring to the boil. Again reduce the amount by half.

5 Stir the garden peas into the cream. Season with salt and pepper and add a squeeze of lemon juice.

6 To serve, place the Dover sole on a large plate and spoon the peas in cream around the fish. Finish with watercress, crispy pancetta and chives.

Try and source small red mullet fillets, larger fillets can be quite overpowering in flavour and that's not want you want for this dish.

GRILLED RED MULLET WITH ROAST PROVENCAL VEGETABLES & AIOLI

Serves 2

Ingredients

1 aubergine
1 long red pepper
2 courgettes
4 tbsp olive oil
1 garlic bulb
Handful of thyme
Handful of rosemary
Sea salt and cracked black pepper
4 small red mullet fillets
25g (1oz) unsalted butter, softened
Juice of 1 lemon
Aioli dressing (see page 205)

To serve

Crunchy bread
Rocket salad

Preparation

1   Make the aioli dressing one day in advance and refrigerate overnight.

Method

1   Preheat the oven to 200°C (400°F/Gas 6) and warm a large roasting tray.

2   Cut the aubergine and the red pepper into quarters, removing the seeds from the pepper. Cut the courgettes into halves, lengthways.

3   Add 2 tbsp of the olive oil to the heated roasting tray. Place all of the vegetables in the tray, making sure that they are covered in olive oil.

4   Cut the garlic bulb in half, break up the cloves and scatter them among the vegetables. Add the thyme and rosemary.

5   Season with salt and pepper and place back in the oven. Roast the vegetables for 30–40 minutes, turning them occasionally, until golden brown.

6   Preheat the grill to hot. Lightly grease a cold baking tray with even amounts of butter and olive oil.

7   Place the red mullet fillets onto the tray, skin side up. Spread the butter and remaining olive oil onto the skin of the fillets.

8   Pour the lemon juice over the fillets and season with salt and pepper.

9   Cook under the grill for 4–5 minutes until golden and cooked through.

10 To serve, spoon the roasted vegetables onto a platter and place the grilled red mullet on top. Drizzle with the aioli dressing and a spoonful of the cooking oil from the vegetables.

11 Serve with crunchy bread and rocket salad leaves.

You can't beat fresh lobster. This simple dish combines the great textures of crunchy fennel, creamy guacamole and sweet meaty lobster.

LOBSTER SALAD WITH MARINATED FENNEL & CHUNKY SPICY GUACAMOLE

Serves 4

Ingredients

2 live lobsters, 450g (1lb) each

2 carrots, peeled and roughly chopped

1 small onion, peeled and roughly chopped

1 leek, trimmed and roughly chopped

1 avocado

½ red onion, peeled and finely diced

1 small red chilli, de-seeded and diced

1 tbsp crème fraîche

2 tsp chopped coriander

Salt and cracked black pepper

2 limes

1 fennel bulb

1 tsp tarragon

1 tsp chervil

1 tsp dill

1 tsp olive oil

Preparation

1   Keep the lobsters in the fridge for 1 hour before cooking so they are in a docile state when the time comes to cook them.

Method

1   Cook the lobsters in a pan of salted boiling water for 7 minutes. Remove from the water and allow to cool.

2   Using a sharp chopping knife, push the tip of the blade into the head until it cuts right through, then cut downwards towards the tail, splitting the body in two. Clean out the head sacks and run the shell under cold water. Take out the tail meats and remove the trail.

3   Slice the tail meats into 1cm (½in) pieces and then place back in the opposite half of the shell to the one you removed the meat from, coloured side up.

4   Crack the claws and remove the meat. Place the meat in the shell of the head.

5   Cut the avocado in half and remove the stone. Peel away the skin and cut into 2.5cm (1in) chunks.

6   Using a fork, roughly mash the avocado and add the red onion, chilli, crème fraîche, coriander and salt and pepper. Finish with the juice of one lime, or to taste.

7   Using a mandoline or a sharp knife, finely slice the fennel. Put in a bowl and add the tarragon, chervil, dill and a squeeze of lime. Add the olive oil and season with salt and pepper. Mix well.

8   To finish, place half a lobster on each dish and accompany with a pile of marinated fennel and a generous spoonful of the avocado guacamole.

SYLVIIS GRACE
JERSEY

J11

LES ECREHOUS

Grill, smoke or BBQ the mackerel – it's up to you!

MACKEREL WITH ENGLISH SALAD & ORANGE, LEMON & GRAIN MUSTARD DRESSING

Serves 4

Special equipment

1 airtight jar

Ingredients

2 oranges

2 lemons

1 tsp grain mustard

4 tbsp olive oil, plus extra for preparing the fish

2 shallots, peeled and sliced into rings

4 whole mackerel, on the bone

Sea salt and cracked black pepper

English salad leaves

1 Granny Smith apple

1   With a sharp knife, remove the skin and pith from the oranges and lemons. Carefully remove the segments from both and retain any juice that's produced.

2   Put 1 tbsp of the orange and lemon juice into a clean jar. Add the mustard and olive oil and screw the lid on. Give the jar a good shake to emulsify the dressing.

3   Add the orange and lemon segments and shallot rings to the jar and allow to infuse for 10–15 minutes.

4   Preheat the grill to high. Top, tail and clean the mackerel. Score the skins, brush with olive oil and season with salt and pepper. Cook for 4–5 minutes on each side or until cooked through.

5   To serve, place the cooked mackerel on a serving platter and arrange the English salad leaves. Core the apple and slice into sticks. Use them to garnish the top of the mackerel and finish by spooning the dressing all over the fish and salad.

This is my interpretation of paella. I add the sliced scallops right at the end so that the heat of the risotto just cooks them lightly.

RISOTTO OF SHELLFISH

Serves 4

Ingredients

900ml (1½ pints) fish stock (see page 207)

2 tbsp olive oil

1 onion, peeled and finely diced

1 garlic clove, peeled and crushed

1 sprig of thyme

1 bay leaf

400g (14oz) risotto rice

100ml (3½fl oz) white wine

1 pinch of saffron

20g (¾oz) unsalted butter

100g (3½oz) cooked peeled prawns

100g (3½oz) cooked shelled mussels

4 scallops, coral removed, sliced

75g (2½oz) cooked peas

1 tbsp coriander

1 tbsp tarragon

1 tbsp chervil

1 tbsp dill

50g (1¾oz) Parmesan cheese, grated

Salt and cracked black pepper

1 Heat the fish stock and keep warm at the side of the stove.

2 In a heavy saucepan add the olive oil, onion, garlic, thyme and bay leaf. Cook on a low heat for about 10 minutes, without colouring the onion, until soft and translucent.

3 Add the rice to the pan and, using a wooden spoon, mix the rice into the onions. You should start to hear the rice crack. Once this happens, add the white wine followed by a ladleful of stock and then the saffron and begin to stir (the secret for a good risotto is lots of steam and lots of stirring). Make sure the rice has fully absorbed the stock before you add another ladle of stock. Continue adding stock until the rice is tender and cooked through.

4 Beat the butter into the rice and add the prawns, mussels and lastly the sliced scallops, peas and herbs. Stir carefully, you're only looking to warm the seafood and slightly cook the scallops.

5 Finish the risotto with some grated Parmesan and season with salt and pepper. Serve straight away.

People always ask me what my favorite meal is, well, here you are.

ROASTED LOBSTER, TRIPLE-COOKED CHIPS & BEARNAISE SAUCE

Serves 2

Special equipment

Deep fat fryer

Ingredients

1 live lobster

About 500ml (16fl oz) vegetable oil, for deep frying

4 large Marfona potatoes, peeled and cut into chunky chips

50g (1¾oz) unsalted butter

Juice of ½ lime

Sea salt

Béarnaise sauce (see page 204)

Preparation

1 Keep the lobster in the fridge for 1 hour before cooking so it is in a docile state when the time comes to cook it.

Method

1 Cook the lobster in a pan of salted boiling water for 6 minutes per 450g (1lb). Remove from the water and allow to cool.

2 To prepare the lobster, pull the claws away from the body. Grip the head and straighten the tail out. On the back of the head there is a small cross. Using a sharp chopping knife, push the tip of the blade into the head until it cuts right through, then cut downwards towards the tail, splitting the body in two. Clean out the lobster head but leave the shell intact. Remove the inside of the tail and clean out the back tube that runs through the meat.

3   To prepare the claws, use the back of a knife to break open the shells and carefully remove the claw and knuckle meat. Put aside.

4   Preheat the oven to 100°C (175°F/lowest Gas). Heat the deep fat fryer to 50°C (90°F). Alternatively, half fill a deep saucepan with the vegetable oil and, using a cooking thermometer, heat to 50°C (90°F).

5   Wash the chips in cold water and dry well in a clean towel.

6   Blanch the chips in the deep fat fryer for 5 minutes. Spoon out onto a tray lined with greaseproof paper.

7   Put the chips in the oven and cook for 20–30 minutes until cooked – check by pushing the tip of a knife through them, they should be soft but still have no colour.

8   Increase the heat on the deep fat fryer or saucepan to 180°C (350°F).

9   Add the butter to a warm frying pan and wait until it starts to foam. Add the lobster and then the lime juice. Take off the heat and leave the lobster meat in the pan to finish cooking through.

10 Place the chips back in the deep fat fryer or saucepan and cook for 4–8 minutes until they are golden brown and crispy. Remove from the oil and drain on kitchen paper.

11 To finish, slice the lobster meat and put back into the shells. Season the chips with salt and serve with Béarnaise sauce.

This is a bit of a show-stopper when you have guests. Open the bags at the table so that everyone gets the full effect of the wonderful aromas.

SEA BASS
EN PAPILLOTE
IN ASIAN AROMATS

Serves 2

Ingredients

2 stalk lemongrass

2 kaffir lime leaf

2 red chillies, de-seeded and chopped

2 tsp green peppercorns

2 tsp peeled and sliced ginger

1 tsp coriander seeds

1 tsp chopped coriander leaves

2 shallots, trimmed and sliced

1 baby bok choi, leaves separated

2 tsp sesame seed oil

90ml (3fl oz) sake

50g (1¾oz) unsalted butter

2 whole sea bass, about 450g (1lb) each

1 Preheat the oven to 180°C (350°F/Gas 4).

2 Bruise the lemongrass stalks to release the flavour. Place them in a large bowl together with the lime leaves, chilli, peppercorns, ginger, coriander seeds and leaves, shallots, bok choi, sesame seed oil, sake and 4 tbsp water and mix.

3 Cut two 30cm (12in) squares of foil. Then cut 2 pieces of greaseproof paper to the same size.

4 Place 1 square of foil on top of each piece of greaseproof paper and fold them both in half, then open out flat again.

5 Spread butter in the middle of each opened foil wrap and lay a sea bass on each. One by one, place the foil wraps in a bowl so the fish is cupped and the liquid won't run out when it is added. Pour half the ingredients from the bowl over and around the fish.

6 Carefully crimp all the edges together to make a sealed bag with the fish inside. Repeat with the remaining ingredients.

7 Place the bags on a baking tray and put in the oven for 10 minutes. The bags will puff right up and the fish will steam.

8 Keep the bags sealed until you are ready to serve, then simply open up and serve in their packaging on plates.

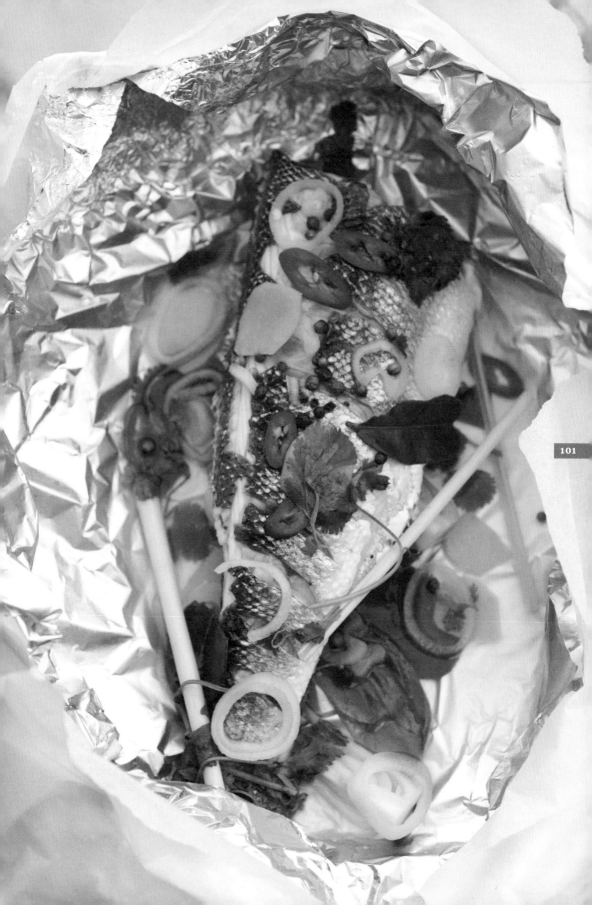

Steaming the sea bass with the lemon butter allows the flavours to infuse and the sweet confit lemon helps intensify the flavour when cooking.

SEA BASS POACHED IN CONFIT LEMON BUTTER WITH ASPARAGUS & ROYAL BAY OYSTERS

Serves 4

Special equipment

Steamer

Ingredients

250g (9oz) unsalted butter

2 lemons

Salt and cracked black pepper

200g (7oz) caster sugar

1 star anise

4 sea bass fillets

8 oysters, removed from their shells and the juice retained

12 asparagus spears

2 tbsp chopped chives

1 To make the confit lemon butter, first put the butter in a bowl and leave to soften.

2 Grate the lemon zest from 1 lemon and squeeze out its juice. Add to the lemon butter and season with salt and pepper. Mix well.

3 Put the caster sugar and 200ml (7fl oz) of water in a saucepan and bring to the boil.

4 Slice the remaining lemon and add to the stock syrup. Add the star anise and cook on a low heat for about 20 minutes, or until the syrup is glossy and translucent. Leave to cool in the pan.

5 For the sea bass, roll out some cling film onto a board, keeping it flat and tight.

6 Place a spoonful of the lemon butter on the cling film; then place a sea bass fillet on top, skin side down.

7 Add a slice of the confit lemon, followed by another spoonful of lemon butter.

8 Fold the cling film over the mixture twice to form a parcel and tuck in the edges to make watertight.

9 Cook in a steamer for 9 minutes.

10 Remove from the steamer and carefully open the parcels at one end using a pair of scissors. Pour the juice into a saucepan and keep warm.

11 Pour the juice from the oysters into another saucepan and warm on a medium heat. Whisk in 1 tsp of lemon butter but do not bring to the boil. Add the oysters to the juice to warm through.

12 Meanwhile, snap the bottoms off the asparagus and steam for 5–6 minutes.

13 To serve, put the asparagus on the plates and place the sea bass on top. Spoon over the oysters and drizzle over some juice from the fish. Finish with a sprinkling of chopped chives.

Sea trout and asparagus complement each other perfectly, as do asparagus and pink grapefruit. Put the three ingredients in a dish together and you get a mind-blowing combination.

SEA TROUT WITH ASPARAGUS & PINK GRAPEFRUIT SABAYON

Serves 4

Ingredients

20g (¾oz) butter
1 pink grapefruit
3 egg yolks
Sea salt and cracked black pepper
1 tbsp chopped chives
4 sea trout steaks
100g (3½oz) unsalted butter, softened
Juice of 1 lemon
Olive oil, to drizzle
12 asparagus spears

Preparation

1 To make clarified butter, put the butter in a heavy saucepan and melt slowly over low heat. Remove the pan from the heat and let stand for 5 minutes.

2 Skim the foam from the top, and slowly pour into a container, discarding the milky solids in the bottom of pan.

Method

1 To make the pink grapefruit sabayon, put 400ml (14fl oz) of water in a saucepan and bring to the boil.

2 Cut the skin and pith from the grapefruit then, using a sharp serrated knife, carefully cut down between the grapefruit segments to remove the segments of fruit. Squeeze the remaining pulp to get all the grapefruit juice and reserve the juice separately.

3 Meanwhile, in a bowl that can sit comfortably over the saucepan of boiling water, combine the egg yolks with 1 tbsp of cold water.

4   Once the water in the saucepan has reached
    boiling point, put the bowl of eggs and water
    on top of it.

5   Using a hand whisk, continuously whisk the
    mixture until the eggs become very light and
    airy. Make sure that you take the bowl off the
    heat every 10 seconds or so to ensure the
    eggs don't scramble. When the mix is four
    times the size of its initial volume, taste it to
    ensure it no longer tastes of egg.

6   Add 1 tbsp of the clarified butter and 2 tbsp
    of the grapefruit juice to the sabayon. Season
    with salt and pepper and finish with the
    chopped chives. Remove from the heat,
    cover with cling film and keep warm.

7   For the sea trout, preheat the grill to hot.

8   Place the sea trout steaks onto a grill tray.
    Season with salt and pepper and, using a
    pastry brush, brush the soft butter over the
    top of each fillet. Then pour over the lemon
    juice followed by a drizzle of olive oil.

9   Place the sea trout steaks under the grill and
    cook for 4–5 minutes. Use a tablespoon to
    spoon any melted butter back onto the fish
    to stop the steaks from drying out.

10 Meanwhile, bring a saucepan of water to the
    boil. Add the asparagus spears and simmer for
    5 minutes or until cooked to your preference.
    Remove from the heat and drain. Remove the
    sea trout steaks from under the grill.

11 To serve, arrange the fish on plates with
    the asparagus spears on top. Garnish with
    pink grapefruit segments and spoon over
    the sabayon sauce.

Cooking turbot, or any flat fish, on the bone is a fantastic method as it helps stop the fish from drying out. Ask your fishmonger to prepare this cut for you. If you can't get hold of turbot then brill is a good alternative.

TRAUNCH OF TURBOT WITH A SMOKED SALMON, HORSERADISH & SPRING PEA SALAD

Serves 4

Ingredients

4 traunches of turbot on the bone with skin left on

Olive oil, for rubbing into the turbot

Salt and cracked black pepper

250g (9oz) smoked salmon

85g (3oz) garden peas, cooked

150g (5½oz) sugar snap peas, cooked

100g (3½oz) broad beans, cooked

50g (1¾oz) watercress

50g (1¾oz) pea shoot leaves

1 tsp of peeled and grated horseradish root

Juice of ½ lemon

2 tbsp crème fraîche

1 tsp chopped chives

1 Heat a griddle pan over a high heat (alternatively you could use a BBQ).

2 Rub some olive oil over the turbot. Season with salt and pepper and place on the hot griddle pan. Coat for about 5 minutes on each side, although this will vary depending on the size of the traunches.

3 Meanwhile, make the salad by tearing up the smoked salmon and mixing with the garden peas, sugar snap peas, broad beans, watercress and pea shoot leaves in a large bowl. Season with salt and pepper.

4 Sprinkle over the horseradish and pour the lemon juice over the salad.

5 In a small bowl, mix together the crème fraîche and chives.

6 When the fish is ready, remove from the heat and serve on plates with a handful of salad and a drizzle of the crème fraîche dressing.

MEAT, GAME & POULTRY

DAVID SCOTT
WHATO PETIT
BEAUREGARD FARM

Sark is a 3 x 1 mile organic island, which is home to 500 inhabitants and more than 200 sheep. To visit Sark is to visit the best of the past; a place without cars and stress, underpinned by a strong sense of community – something that perhaps we've lost sight of in the modern world.

Sark sheep are free to roam anywhere in the island and are often found on the headland. Sark is reputed to be one of the best environments to rear sheep and the diverse nature of their diet, thanks to their liberal grazing, leads to the meat having incredible flavour.

According to farmer David Scott, the best time to eat the lamb is in the spring when the sheep have enjoyed the salty headlands laden with wild herbs and clovers, after their tough fight against the winter months. He fully believes that the stress-free life the sheep enjoy adds to the flavour of the lamb.

I was brought up on plate pies. My mum would always bake on a Sunday afternoon using whatever was left over from lunch. You would think after cooking such a big Sunday roast she might have wanted to put her feet up, but not mum.

CHICKEN, LEEK & MUSHROOM PLATE PIE

Serves 4

Special equipment

23cm (9in) diameter deep pie plate

Ingredients

1 tbsp olive oil

100g (3½oz) leeks, trimmed and sliced

115g (4oz) brown cap mushrooms

400ml (14fl oz) chicken stock (see page 207)

300ml (10fl oz) double cream

400g (14oz) cooked chicken pieces

1 tbsp roughly chopped tarragon

Salt and cracked black pepper

350g (12oz) ready-rolled puff pastry sheets

1 egg, beaten

1 Preheat the oven to 200°C (400°F/Gas 6).

2 Heat the olive oil in a large saucepan over a medium heat. Add the leeks and cook for 1 minute.

3 Add the mushrooms and cook for another minute.

4 Add the chicken stock and double cream to the pan. Bring to the boil and reduce the liquid until it starts to thicken slightly.

5 Then add the chicken pieces and tarragon. Season with salt and pepper and stir thoroughly.

6 Once the chicken has heated through, remove from the heat and spoon the pie mixture into the pie plate, filling it right up.

7 Cut out the pastry to size so that it will cover your dish and then lay it on top. Cut around the side of the plate to remove excess and then crimp the pastry at the edges to seal the dish.

8 Brush the egg wash over the pastry to glaze.

9 Place the dish in the oven and bake for 30 minutes, or until golden brown and the pastry has cooked.

10 When ready, remove from the oven and serve immediately.

113

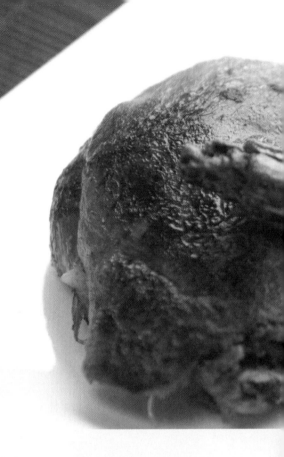

This recipe needs to be prepared at least 24 hours in advance. The beauty of cooking like this is that the legs are submerged in the goose fat and, if stored properly in the fridge, they will last for up to 2 weeks.

This is a very old French method of cooking and storing food – and it's extremely good!

CONFIT OF DUCK LEGS WITH VANILLA & SPICED KUMQUAT CHUTNEY

Serves 4

Special equipment

Food processor

Ingredients

10 shallots, peeled and sliced
5 garlic cloves, peeled and sliced
2 sprigs of thyme
2 sprigs of rosemary
2 bay leaves
¼ lemon, sliced
150g (5½oz) sea salt
75g (2½oz) caster sugar
10 black peppercorns
4 juniper berries
2 cloves
½ star anise
100ml (3½fl oz) olive oil
4 duck legs
300g (10oz) goose fat
Kumquat chutney (see page 208)

Preparation

1 Preheat the oven to 200°C (400°F/Gas 6).

2 Place all of the ingredients, accept the duck legs, goose fat and chutney, in a roasting tray and mix well. Roast in the oven for 15 minutes or until soft and golden brown.

3 Using a food processor, liquidise the mixture until smooth and allow to cool.

4 Rub the mix into each of the duck legs very well, leaving a nice coating of the mixture on the legs.

5 Place the legs in a container pressing them together. If there is any confit mixture left, smooth over the top of the legs.

6 Cover with cling film and marinate in the fridge for at least 24 hours but 3–4 days would be ideal as this allows the confit mix to really penetrate the leg meat.

Method

1 Preheat the oven to 100°C (210°F/lowest Gas).

2 Wash the duck legs in cold water removing all of the mixture and pat dry with a clean cloth.

3 Place them in a deep roasting tray and cover with the goose fat.

4 Put in the oven and cook for 3 hours or until the meat falls away from the bone.

5 When cooked, you can either finish them straight away or store in the fridge.

6 To store, let the legs cool right down in the goose fat until they are cold enough to put in the fridge. They can remain in the fridge for up to 2 weeks.

7 To finish, preheat the oven to 180°C (350°F/ Gas 4) and carefully remove the legs from the goose fat using a slotted spoon. Place on a roasting tray, skin side down, and put them back in the oven for 20 minutes until the skin turns golden brown and crispy. Serve the duck legs hot with the kumquat chutney.

I always think coq au vin is even better in flavour when it's reheated the next day. Serve it with buttery mashed potato for a real comfort dish.

MY COQ AU VIN

Serves 4

Ingredients

4 chicken legs

500ml (16fl oz) red wine

4 garlic cloves, peeled

200g (7oz) plain flour, lightly seasoned with salt and pepper

3 tbsp olive oil

2 slices smoked bacon, diced

1 onion, peeled and cut into quarters

1 carrot, peeled and roughly diced

1 leek, trimmed and roughly diced

1 celery stick, roughly diced

1 sprig of thyme

1 sprig of rosemary

1 bay leaf

1 tbsp demerara sugar

1 tbsp tomato purée

500ml (16fl oz) chicken stock (see page 207)

6 small shallots, peeled

300g (10oz) pancetta lardons

200g (7oz) button mushrooms

Bunch of flat-leaf parsley, chopped

Preparation

1   Cut the chicken legs in half through the knee joint to separate the drumstick from the thigh and place in a large bowl.

2   Pour over the red wine, add the garlic and cover with cling film. Place in the fridge and marinate overnight.

Method

1   Preheat the oven to 110°C (230°F/lowest Gas).

2   Remove the chicken from the red wine and pat dry with a clean towel. Reserve the wine marinade and garlic cloves for cooking.

3   Dust the chicken legs with the seasoned flour and tap off any excess.

4   Fry the legs in a saucepan with 1 tbsp of the olive oil until golden brown on all sides. Remove from the pan.

5   Add the smoked bacon to the pan and allow the bacon to gain some colour before adding the onion, carrot, leek, celery, garlic, thyme, rosemary and bay leaf. Cook for 2–3 minutes, allowing the vegetables to turn golden brown.

6   Add the demerara sugar and tomato purée and cook for a further 3 minutes, stirring well.

7   Add the red wine that you marinated the chicken in and the chicken stock to the pan and bring to the boil.

8   Place the chicken legs back into the pan, submerging them in the liquid.

9   Cover the pan with a lid or foil and cook in the oven for 1½ hours. Remove the pan from the oven and set aside and keep warm.

10 Turn the oven up to 200°C (400°F/Gas 6). Take a shallow baking tray and add the shallots, pancetta lardons and drizzle with 2 tbsp olive oil. Roast in the oven for 10 minutes. Add the button mushrooms and roast for a further 10 minutes.

11 To serve, spoon the chicken into a serving bowl and garnish with the roast shallots, button mushrooms and pancetta. Pour over the cooking liquid and sprinkle with the chopped parsley.

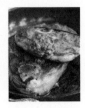

This lamb dish makes a simple but delicious lunch or dinner. Make sure you use good quality fresh anchovies for the butter. It is best served with roasted red onions.

PAN-ROASTED LAMB LEG CHOPS WITH CAPER, PARSLEY, MINT & ANCHOVY BUTTER

Serves 2

Ingredients

10 tbsp olive oil

4 garlic cloves, peeled

2 sprigs of rosemary

2 sprigs of thyme

Sea salt and cracked black pepper

2 lamb gigot steaks

50g (1½oz) unsalted butter, softened

Small handful of mint leaves, finely chopped

1 tsp baby capers, roughly chopped

2 tsp finely chopped anchovies

Preparation

1 Pour the olive oil onto a baking tray.

2 Add the garlic, rosemary, thyme and salt and pepper.

3 Place the lamb steaks in the tray, cover with cling film and refrigerate for 1 day.

4 For the anchovy butter, place the remaining ingredients in a bowl and mix together well.

5 Spoon the mixture onto a piece of cling film. Using the cling film, roll up the butter into a cylindrical shape. Tie the ends in knots and place in the fridge to firm up.

Method

1 Preheat the grill to hot and warm a baking tray.

2 Heat a large griddle pan over a high heat until piping hot.

3 Remove the tray of lamb steaks from the fridge. Drain off the oil and reserve.

4 Heat a griddle to hot with some of the marinating oil. Sear the lamb steaks on both sides until golden brown. Remove from heat and set aside.

5 Remove the anchovy butter from the fridge. Take off the cling film and, on a clean board, cut the butter into 1cm (½in) thick slices.

6 Put the lamb steaks on the preheated baking tray, place the butter slices on top of the steaks and then place the tray under the hot grill.

7 As soon as the butter starts to melt, remove from the grill and serve.

Game season is always a highlight of the year for me. You can make the orange and onion marmalade well in advance and it will keep in the fridge in an airtight container for up to 4 weeks.

ROAST PHEASANT WITH ORANGE & ONION MARMALADE & JUICES

Serves 2

Ingredients

1 large orange
1 large onion, peeled and roughly chopped
4 tbsp white wine vinegar
100g (3½oz) demerara sugar
2 tbsp Cointreau
½ cinnamon stick
1 blade of mace
1 tsp coriander seeds
5 all-spice berries, crushed
2 bacon rashers, sliced
1 sprig of thyme
1 sprig of rosemary
1 bay leaf
1 oven-ready pheasant
250ml (8fl oz) chicken stock (see page 207)

1 Preheat the oven to 140°C (275°F/Gas 1).

2 Cut the orange into quarters, de-seed and then thinly slice.

3 Transfer onto a roasting tray and add the onion. Mix together thoroughly.

4 Put the vinegar, sugar, 1 tbsp of the Cointreau, cinnamon, mace, coriander seeds and spice berries into a saucepan. Bring to the boil and continue to boil for 3 minutes. Sieve the liquid over the sliced oranges and onions and discard the spices.

5 Cover with foil and cook for 3½ hours, stirring occasionally. The oranges and onions will eventually caramelise. Be careful not to over cook, as this will cause the mixture to turn solid.

6 Remove from the oven and allow to cool before storing.

7 Turn the oven up to 170°C (340°F/Gas 4).

8 Lay the bacon, thyme, rosemary and bay leaf over the pheasant and roast in the oven for 20 minutes. Remove from the oven and turn the pheasant upside down to allow the juices to flow back through the breasts. Rest for about 8 minutes before serving.

9 Meanwhile, add the remaining Cointreau and the chicken stock to the roasting tray and bring to the boil on the hob. Pass through a sieve and then serve with the pheasant.

This is a fantastic way to cook rabbit. Steaming the loin keeps all the moisture and delicious juices in.

ROAST RABBIT LOIN IN PANCETTA WITH MOROCCAN-STYLE COUSCOUS & CALAMARI

Serves 2

Special equipment

Steamer

Ingredients

1 whole rabbit loin, cleaned

6 slices of pancetta or Parma ham

200ml (7fl oz) chicken stock (see page 207)

150g (5½oz) couscous

3 tbsp olive oil

2 tbsp mixed herbs (dill, tarragon, coriander)

20g (¾oz) black olives, pitted and sliced

20g (¾oz) sun-blushed tomatoes, halved

20g (¾oz) pine nuts, toasted

½ lemon

Sea salt and cracked black pepper

50g (1¾oz) calamari strips, cleaned

20g (¾oz) unsalted butter

1. With a sharp knife, carefully remove the two loin fillets from the saddle by running the knife down close to the backbone. Trim off any sinew, so that you are left with two clean fillets.

2. Lay the loin fillets side by side, top to tail, so they form an even shape together.

3. Carefully wrap the pancetta or Parma ham around both the loin fillets, making sure you overlap the slices so the fillets are covered and are in a single piece.

4. Lay some cling film on a flat surface, place the covered loin 5cm (2in) from one edge of the cling film and then roll it up tight so that you create a sausage shape. Tie the cling film in knots at both ends, forcing any air out.

5. Warm the chicken stock in a saucepan.

6. Place the couscous grains in a bowl and pour over the hot chicken stock. Cover the bowl with cling film and leave in a warm place for 15 minutes.

7   To finish the couscous, run a fork through to break up the grains and add 1 tbsp of the olive oil together with the mixed herbs, black olives, sun blushed tomatoes and toasted pine nuts. Finish with a squeeze of lemon juice and season with salt and pepper. Keep warm.

8   Place the rolled loin in the steamer for 4 minutes. Remove from the steamer and, once cool enough to touch, carefully remove the cling film.

9   In a medium frying pan, heat 1 tbsp of the olive oil. Add the rabbit fillet roll and cook for 2 minutes, or until the pancetta turns golden brown.

10   Add the remaining 1 tbsp of olive oil to a separate hot pan. Add the calamari strips and fry quickly for 20 seconds. Remove from the heat.

11   Cut the rabbit loin into slices about 1cm (½in) thick.

12   Melt the butter and add a good squeeze of lemon juice. Keep warm.

13   To serve, spoon the warm couscous onto 2 plates and arrange the rabbit on top. Add the calamari to the dish and drizzle with the lemon butter. Season with salt and pepper.

125

Ask your butcher to score the pork for you. Scoring will help create fantastically crispy crackling.

ROAST RACK OF PORK WITH BAKED APPLES & SOFT PARMESAN POLENTA

Serves 4

Ingredients

1 large potato, peeled

1.8kg (4lb) rack of pork, skin scored

Olive oil, for drizzling

1 tsp sea salt

175g (6oz) unsalted butter

1 litre (1¾ pints) hot water

400ml (14fl oz) milk

140g (5oz) polenta

Sea salt and cracked black pepper

70g (2½oz) unsalted butter

80g (3oz) Parmesan cheese, grated

4 Granny Smith apples

Handful of sage

Madeira sauce (see page 205)

1 Preheat the oven to 170°C (350°F/Gas 4).

2 Slice the potato lengthways into three and place on the bottom of a roasting tray.

3 Sit the pork rack on top of the potato.

4 Drizzle some olive oil all over the skin of the pork. Sprinkle with the salt and rub into the scored skin with your hands.

5 Place in the oven and roast for 1–1½ hours (about 18–20 minutes per 450g/1lb).

6 While the pork is roasting, make the Parmesan polenta. Put the hot water and milk in a saucepan and bring to the boil over a high heat.

7 Reduce the heat and simmer while you slowly pour in the polenta. Gently whisk to combine the mixture.

8 Cook for about 25 minutes, stirring frequently, until the polenta has swollen and the liquid has been absorbed.

9 Once cooked, season with salt and pepper. Stir in 75g (2½oz) of the butter and then the Parmesan cheese. Keep warm until needed.

10 About 15 minutes before the pork is ready, cut the apples in half but leave the cores and skin on. Remove the roasting tray containing the pork from the oven and add the remaining butter to it. Increase the oven temperature to 200°C (400°F/Gas 6).

11 Place the apples around the meat and then sprinkle over the sage leaves. Put the roasting tray back in the oven and cook for the remaining 15 minutes.

12 When ready, remove the pork from the oven. The apples should be golden and soft. Remove them from the roasting tray and set aside for serving.

13 Allow the pork to rest for at least 20 minutes. Discard the potato.

14 To finish, place the pork on a large platter with the baked apples around it. Pour the sage butter cooking juices over the top. Serve with the soft polenta and Madeira sauce.

If you have some chocolate in the cupboard, grate it over the top of this dish. Chocolate adds another dynamic and it's great with venison.

ROAST VENISON LOIN WITH PARSNIPS, CARDAMOM - SCENTED QUINOA & MEDJOOL DATES

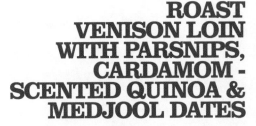

Serves 2

Ingredients

100g (3½oz) quinoa

200ml (7fl oz) chicken stock (see page 207)

5 whole cardamom pods

1 garlic clove, peeled

1 sprig of thyme

2 parsnips, peeled and cut into quarters

4 tbsp olive oil

1 tbsp maple syrup

250g (9oz) venison loin, trimmed and cleaned

Salt and cracked black pepper

25g (1oz) unsalted butter

6 medjool dates

1 tbsp cooked and diced baby carrots

1 tsp peeled and grated ginger

1 tsp chopped coriander

Madeira sauce (see page 205)

1   Preheat the oven to 170°C (340°F/Gas 4).

2   Place the quinoa in a saucepan and cover with the chicken stock. Add the cardamom pods, garlic and thyme, bring to the boil then reduce the heat and let the mixture simmer for 12–15 minutes – the grains should have split open and be tender.

3   Remove the cardamom pods, garlic clove and thyme stalk and discard. Put the quinoa aside in its pan.

4   Warm a roasting tray in the oven.

5   Cook the parsnips in salted boiling water for 15 minutes or until just cooked.

6   Remove from the water and place in the hot roasting tray from the oven with 2 tbsp of the olive oil. Put the roasting tray back into the oven and cook the parsnips for 6–8 minutes, or until golden brown turning them every 2 minutes.

7 When the parsnips are golden brown, add the maple syrup and place back in the oven for a further 2 minutes so the maple syrup glazes the parsnips. Keep warm until needed.

8 Heat a frying pan until very hot and add the remaining 2 tbsp of olive oil.

9 Season the venison loin with salt and pepper and put straight into the pan. Seal the venison on all sides until golden brown.

10 Add the butter to the pan. When it starts to foam, turn down the heat to stop the butter from burning and cook for a further 2 minutes, continuously rolling the loin in the butter. (If you prefer the venison well cooked, allow another 4–5 minutes cooking time.) Remove from the pan.

11 Meanwhile, warm the quinoa through. Chop 4 of the dates and add them to the pan along with the carrots, ginger and coriander. Season with salt and pepper and mix well.

12 To serve, spoon the quinoa onto 2 plates. Carve the venison loin and lay on top and garnish with the remaining dates. Add the roast glazed parsnips and finish the whole dish with the Madeira sauce.

This is such a good way to cook lamb. The flavour of the hay is so apparent when you eat it and by adding the garlic, lavender and fresh herbs, you really enhance it. The hay also helps to keep the meat nice and moist.

SHOULDER OF LAMB COOKED IN HAY WITH LAVENDER, HERBS & GARLIC

Serves 6

Ingredients

A small bag of long cut hay (enough to cover the shoulder of lamb)

4 garlic bulbs

1 shoulder of lamb, bone removed and tied, 1.35kg (3lb) finished weight

Bunch of thyme

Bunch of rosemary

Sea salt and cracked black pepper

Small bunch of lavender

1 Soak the hay in water for about 5 minutes.

2 Preheat the oven to 180°C (350°F/Gas 4).

3 Take one of the garlic bulbs, separate the cloves, peel them and then cut in half.

4 With a sharp knife, pierce the shoulder of lamb ten times all over, making holes big enough to inset the halved garlic cloves.

5 Insert a garlic half and small sprig of thyme and rosemary into each of the holes you have made in the shoulder of lamb. You don't need to use all the herbs as the rest will be used when cooking the lamb. Season the joint with salt and pepper.

6 Wring the water out of the hay and place half of it in the bottom of a roasting tray large enough for the shoulder of lamb. Then place the lamb shoulder on top of the hay.

7 Cut the remaining garlic bulbs in half (there's no need to peel them). Then place them in the hay surrounding the lamb, along with the lavender and remaining thyme and rosemary sprigs.

8 Cover the lamb with the rest of the hay so the shoulder is totally covered.

9 Place in the oven and cook for 45 minutes. Remove the top layer of hay from the lamb and cook for a further 30 minutes, or until the joint gains a nice golden brown.

10 When ready, remove from the oven and allow the lamb to rest in the hay for 10–15 minutes before serving.

I've messed around with cooking belly pork in so many ways over the years, but this way has to be the best.

SLOW-COOKED BELLY PORK GLAZED WITH HONEY & GRAIN MUSTARD

Serves 6

Ingredients

500g (1lb 2oz) sea salt

500g (1lb 2oz) caster sugar

1 tsp cayenne pepper

Bunch of thyme

8 garlic cloves, peeled and sliced

Bunch of rosemary

1.35kg (3lb) pork belly, whole with rib bones removed and rind scored

2 litres (3½ pints) sunflower oil

50g (1¾oz) honey

50g (1¾oz) wholegrain mustard

Mushrooms a la grecque (see page 209)

Sweet pickled duck eggs (see page 209)

Preparation

1 In a large bowl, mix together the salt, sugar and cayenne pepper.

2 Sprinkle half the salt mix onto the bottom of a deep-sided roasting tray ensuring the base is totally covered. Take half the thyme, garlic and rosemary and sprinkle liberally over the salt.

3 Lay the pork belly on top.

4 Repeat the process but this time cover the top of the pork with the salt mix, making sure the meat is well covered. Then sprinkle with the remaining herbs and garlic.

5 Cover with cling film and cure in the fridge for at least 12 hours.

Method

1 Preheat the oven to 100°C (210°F/lowest Gas).

2 Wash the salt mix off the pork belly and dry the meat.

3 Lay the pork belly back into a clean deep-sided roasting tray. Pour over the oil, ensuring that it totally covers the meat.

4 Cover with foil, or a lid if you have one that fits the tray. Place in the oven and cook for 2 hours.

5 Remove the pork from the oil and place on a clean tray. Turn the oven up to 170°C (340°F/Gas 4).

6 In a separate bowl, mix together the honey and mustard. Spread the mixture evenly on top of the pork belly and then place back in the oven for a further 30 minutes, or until it is golden brown.

7 Serve with mushrooms a la grecque and sweet pickled duck eggs.

135

My tip for this recipe is to add herbs and garlic to the shanks and stock after you've braised them, which allows the stock to take on these fantastic fresh flavours.

SLOW-COOKED LAMB SHANK, SPRING VEGETABLES & BASIL BROTH

Serves 2

Ingredients

3 tbsp olive oil, plus extra for drizzling

2 lamb shanks, trimmed and tied

Salt and cracked black pepper

1 litre (1¾ pints) chicken stock (see page 207)

2 garlic bulbs

Handful of thyme

Handful of rosemary

2 tbsp spring peas

8 baby plum tomatoes

2 tbsp broad beans, skins removed

4 spring onions, trimmed and sliced

1 courgette, trimmed and sliced

6 basil leaves, roughly torn

1 tbsp basil pesto

1 Preheat the oven to 140°C (275°F/Gas 1).

2 Heat a heavy ovenproof dish over a medium heat and add the olive oil.

3 Meanwhile, season the lamb shanks with salt and pepper.

4 Place the shanks into the pan and brown on all sides.

5 Add the chicken stock to the pan along with one of the garlic bulbs and half of the thyme and rosemary. Bring to the boil.

6 Cover with a lid or foil and place in the oven for 2 hours, or until the meat falls from the bone.

7 Remove the dish from the oven and set aside.

8 Add the rest of the garlic, thyme and rosemary to the dish, re-cover and leave to stand for about 15 minutes for the flavours to infuse.

9 Strain the cooking liquid into a large saucepan and bring to the boil.

10 Add the peas, tomatoes, broad beans, spring onions and courgette to the pan and cook for 1 minute.

11 Remove the lamb shanks from the dish and place onto serving plates.

12 Spoon the stock and vegetables over the lamb shanks, drizzle with olive oil, sprinkle over the basil leaves and finish with a spoonful of pesto.

THE PERFECT SUNDAY ROAST

I grew up in the north east of England and back then before Sunday lunch the man of the house would always eat his Yorkshire pudding with onion gravy. I enjoy a good Sunday lunch with my family now, but we eat everything all at once and all together!

THE PERFECT SUNDAY ROAST

Serves 8

Ingredients

4 bone rib of beef

2 tbsp beef dripping

Sea salt and cracked black pepper

1   Preheat the oven to 180°C (350°F/Gas 4).

2   Place the beef in a roasting tray. Spread the beef dripping over the meat and season with salt and pepper.

3   Roast in the oven, allowing 15 minutes per 450g (1lb), plus an additional 15 minutes for a medium finish. For rare, cook for 10 minutes per 450g (1lb), plus an additional 10 minutes; and for well done, cook for 20 minutes per 450g (1lb), plus an additional 20 minutes.

4   When cooked, remove from the oven and rest for around 15 minutes before serving.

YORKSHIRE PUDDING WITH ONION GRAVY

Serves 8

Ingredients

4 large eggs
250ml (8fl oz) milk
250g (9oz) plain flour
Salt and cracked black pepper
2 sprigs of thyme
1 tbsp beef dripping
Onion gravy (see page 208)

Preparation

1 Crack the eggs into a bowl and add the milk. Sift in the flour and whisk well.

2 Pour the mix through a fine sieve into a clean bowl. Season with salt and cracked black pepper.

3 Scrape the thyme leaves from the stems and add the leaves to the batter mixture. Stir well, cover with cling film and leave in the fridge for 24 hours.

Method

1 Remove the batter mix from the fridge about 30 minutes before you need to use it and stir well.

2 Preheat the oven to 220°C (425°F/Gas 7) and heat a 24 x 12cm (10 x 5in) deep Yorkshire pudding tin until very hot.

3 Add the beef dripping to the tin and place back in the oven for a further 5 minutes.

4 Pour the Yorkshire pudding mix into the hot fat in the tin. Put back in the oven straight away.

5 Cook in the oven for about 15 minutes, or until golden brown and doubled in size. Then turn down the oven to 120°C (235°F/ lowest Gas) and cook for a further 5 minutes.

6 Serve with lashings of onion gravy.

THE PERFECT
SUNDAY ROAST

ROAST POTATOES
WITH THYME

Ingredients

1.5kg (3lb 3oz) Maris Piper potatoes

Sea salt and
cracked black pepper

4 tbsp duck fat

2 tsp chopped thyme

1   Preheat the oven to 180°C (350°F/Gas 4) and place a deep-sided roasting tray inside.

2   Peel and cut the potatoes in half and rinse in cold running water to take away the starch.

3   Place in a saucepan and cover with cold water. Add a good pinch of salt and bring to the boil.

4   Once the potatoes are boiling, simmer for about 15 minutes or until nearly cooked. Next, carefully drain the water and leave the potatoes in the saucepan to steam. The edges will start to fall and break away.

5   Add the duck fat to the preheated roasting tray. Place back into the oven until the fat is very hot.

6   Carefully spoon the potatoes into the hot fat, making sure you cover all the potatoes in the fat. Place the tray back in the oven and cook for 35–40 minutes turning occasionally. Add more duck fat if needed.

7   Remove from the oven once golden and crispy and finish with pepper and thyme.

ROAST RED ONIONS IN THEIR SKINS

Ingredients

4 tbsp olive oil

4 red onions, peeled and cut in half through the root

2 garlic bulbs, cut in half

4 sprigs of thyme

4 sprigs of rosemary

Sea salt and cracked black pepper

1 Preheat the oven to 180°C (350°F/Gas 4)

2 Add 2 tbsp of the olive oil to a hot frying pan and add the red onions, flat side down. Fry for about 2 minutes or until golden brown and then remove from the pan.

3 Lay a sheet of foil over a baking tray and place the red onions on top. Add the garlic, thyme, rosemary and the remaining olive oil and season with salt and pepper. Cover with more foil. Cook in the oven for 30 minutes or until soft.

ROAST CARROTS WITH ROSEMARY & CARDAMOM

Ingredients

1.8kg (4lb) small sweet carrots, peeled

100g (3½oz) unsalted butter

6 cardamom pods

2 tsp rosemary

Sea salt and cracked black pepper

1 Place the carrots into a large saucepan and cover with salted water.

2 Bring to the boil over a high heat and cook for 15 minutes until tender, making sure they still have a slight crunch to them.

3 In a hot pan add the butter and wait for it to begin to foam. Drop in the carrots, cardamom pods and rosemary and cook for 3 minutes until slightly golden.

4 Season to taste with salt and pepper.

TENDER-STEM BROCCOLI WITH GARLIC

Ingredients

500g (1lb 2oz) tender-stem or purple sprouting broccoli

3 tsp olive oil

4 shallots, peeled and sliced

2 garlic cloves, peeled and chopped

Sea salt and cracked black pepper

1 Cook the broccoli in boiling salted water for 3 minutes and drain well.

2 Heat the olive oil in a frying pan and add the shallots and garlic. Cook for 20 seconds before adding the broccoli. Cook for a further 20 seconds and season with salt and pepper.

PASTA & VEGETARIAN

FENELLA MADDISON TORTEVAL CHEESE

Born in Sussex, but very much adopted by islanders, Fenella is a well recognised character in Guernsey. Even more famous is her cheese, though, which is made from locally sourced cow and goat's milk.

Fenella is an artisan cheese maker, making her unique cheese by hand. This, in my opinion, gives the cheese a better flavour, and it's a general consensus because Fenella's cheeses have won awards at the Nantwich International Cheese Show and at The World Cheese awards.

Dairy farming is still a huge part of the farming industry across all the islands and the creamy milk produced here helps to create some of the best tasting cheeses and cream in the UK.

The Fort Grey cheese I use is made by Fenella on the island of Guernsey. She makes her cheese from pure Guernsey milk, which has a high fat content, and this is why I have only allowed just 1 minute in this recipe for the cheese to cook.

ASPARAGUS, ROAST RED ONION & FORT GREY CHEESE TARTS

Serves 2

Special equipment

Two 10cm (4in) diameter individual tart cases

Dry rice or baking beans

Ingredients

400g (14oz) plain flour

Pinch of salt

200g (7oz) unsalted butter, cold and diced

3 eggs

1 tsp milk

100ml (3½fl oz) double cream

1 tsp chives, chopped

Salt and cracked black pepper

4 asparagus spears

½ roast red onion in its skin (see page 143)

4 slices Fort Grey blue cheese (or a good blue cheese)

40g (1¼oz) rocket salad

Olive oil and balsamic vinegar, to serve

1   To make the pastry, sift the flour and salt into a mixing bowl and add the diced butter. Using your fingers, rub the butter into the flour until it resembles breadcrumbs.

2   Add 1 egg, mix well, and then add a little iced water until the pastry comes together. Make sure the pastry is not too dry as it will fall apart when rolling out. Wrap the pastry in cling film and rest in the fridge for 20–30 minutes before rolling out.

3   Preheat the oven to 170°C (340°F/Gas 4).

4   Roll out the pastry to 4mm (¼in) thickness. Line the individual tart cases with the pastry, making sure the pastry goes right into the edge of the cases.

5   Cover the pastry with cling film then fill with dry rice or baking beans. Bake in the oven for 15 minutes then remove the cling film and rice/baking beans.

6   Whisk 1 egg with the milk and egg brush the wash over the tarts. Place back in the oven for 2 minutes, or until golden brown. Remove from the oven and turn up the oven to 190°C (375°F/Gas 5).

7   Crack 1 egg into a bowl and whisk together with the double cream and chopped chives and season with salt and pepper.

8   Lay the asparagus tips in the tarts and add the roast red onion petals.

9   Carefully pour the quiche mixture on top.

10 Place in the oven and cook for 10 minutes, or until set.

11 Remove from the oven and place the Fort Grey cheese slices on top of the tarts. Place back in the oven for 1 minute, or until the cheese just melts.

12 Serve warm with the rocket salad drizzled with olive oil and balsamic vinegar.

This method of making soufflé takes the stress out of this notoriously tricky dish.

CHEESE SOUFFLE WITH APPLE, WALNUT & POMEGRANATE SALAD

Serves 4

Special equipment

Four 10cm (4in) diameter ovenproof moulds/ramekins

Steamer

Ingredients

240ml (8fl oz) milk

3 tbsp plain flour

60g (2oz) butter, unsalted

6 eggs, separated

175g (6oz) mature cheddar cheese, grated

1 tbsp chopped chives

Sea salt and cracked black pepper

5 tbsp grated Parmesan cheese

2 red apples, cored and cut into eighths

6 tbsp whole walnuts

150g (5½oz) rocket salad

6 tbsp pomegranate seeds

2 tsp walnut oil, for dressing

1 Pour the milk into a saucepan and warm gently over a low heat (just so you take the chill off it).

2 Sift the flour into the milk and mix well.

3 Cook on a moderate heat until you can no longer taste the flour in the mixture and there are no lumps.

4 Remove from the heat.

5 Beat the butter into the flour.

6 Beat the egg yolks into the mix, then add the cheddar cheese.

7 Add the chopped chives and season with salt and pepper.

8 Grease the moulds/ramekins with soft butter and line with the grated Parmesan cheese.

9 Whisk up the egg whites in a medium size bowl until you have firm peaks.

10 Carefully fold the egg whites into the cheese sauce, taking care not to deflate them by over-working or being too heavy handed.

11 Spoon the mixture into the moulds and cook in a steamer for 12 minutes.

12 When cooked, remove from the steamer and leave to stand for 10 minutes or until they are cool enough to handle.

13 Remove the soufflés from the moulds. At this stage, you can either put them in the fridge until needed or re-cook straight away in a preheated oven at 200°C (400°F/Gas 6) on a baking tray lined with greaseproof paper for 6–8 minutes.

14 To serve, arrange the apple on the plates with the walnuts, rocket salad and pomegranate seeds. Remove the soufflés from the oven and place straight onto the salad. Drizzle with walnut oil and serve straight away.

I love fresh gnocchi. Served with new season broad beans and the Pecorino cheese, it's a wonderful combination. Make sure you source the 00 flour as this gives the gnocchi its light texture.

HERB GNOCCHI WITH BROAD BEANS & PECORINO

Serves 2

Ingredients

2 Marfona potatoes
140g (5oz) broad beans
90g (3oz) 00 flour
2 egg yolks
2 tsp chopped dill
2 tsp chopped tarragon
2 tsp chopped chives
Salt and cracked black pepper
50g (1¾oz) unsalted butter
100g (3½oz) Pecorino cheese shavings
50g (1¾oz) rocket salad
50g (1¾oz) pea shoots
1 tsp hazelnut oil

1   Preheat the oven to 170°C (340°F/Gas 4).

2   Bake the potatoes for about 1 hour or until cooked through. Check by pushing the tip of a knife into the potatoes.

3   Blanche the broad beans for 2 minutes in boiling salted water and then plunge into cold water. When cool, peel off the skins.

4   While they are still hot, cut them in half and scoop out the insides into a clean, dry bowl. Discard the skins.

5   Using a fork, break up the potatoes and allow to cool slightly.

6   Sift the flour over the potato and use your hands to mix in well. Next add the egg yolks, followed by the herbs and then season with salt and pepper.

7   Roll out the dough into long sausage shapes approximately 1cm (½in) thick. With a sharp knife cut into 2.5cm (1in) dumplings.

8   Bring a pan of salted water to the boil and drop in the gnocchi. Cook for 2 minutes, remove them with a slotted spoon and put into iced water to stop the cooking. Drain well on kitchen paper.

9   Melt the butter in a frying pan and once it starts to foam, add the gnocchi and cook for 1 minute. The gnocchi should take on a slightly nut brown color.

10 Reheat the broad beans in boiling salted water.

11 To serve, divide the gnocchi between 2 plates, scatter over the broad beans and shavings of Pecorino cheese. Finish by adding the rocket and pea shoots and a drizzle of hazelnut oil.

155

SEIGNEURIE GARDENS, SARK

This method of cooking mussels is similar to a classic moules marinière but I only use white wine in this recipe because when the mussels open, the meat takes on a fantastic flavour.

LINGUINE WITH MUSSELS, CHORIZO, TOMATO & HERB VIERGE

Serves 2

Ingredients

1kg (2¼lb) mussels, in their shell
75ml (2½fl oz) white wine
200g (7oz) fresh linguine pasta
Salt and cracked black pepper
2 tbsp olive oil
100g (3½oz) chorizo sausage, skinned and sliced
2 shallots, peeled and sliced
1 tsp dill
1 tsp chopped chives
1 tsp chopped coriander
6 baby plum tomatoes, quartered and seeds removed
1 tsp lemon juice

1 Heat a large saucepan and add the mussels. Pour in the white wine and cover with a lid. Cook for 2 minutes or until the shells have opened.

2 Remove from the heat and leave to cool slightly before removing the meat from the shells, discarding any that have remained closed during cooking.

3 Bring a pan of salted water to the boil and cook the linguine for 3 minutes. Strain through a colander and then place the linguine back in the pan. Season with salt and pepper and drizzle with 1 tbsp of the olive oil to stop the pasta from sticking together. Cover the pan with cling film until you are ready to serve.

4 For the herb vierge, warm the remaining 1 tbsp of olive oil in a frying pan and add the mussels and sliced chorizo and allow to warm through.

5 Add the shallots, herbs and plum tomatoes and cook for a further 2 minutes. Season with salt, pepper and the lemon juice.

6 To serve, twirl a large fork into the linguine to produce a cone of pasta. Slide off carefully onto a serving plate and spoon over the mussels, chorizo and herb vierge.

Wild garlic is at its best during spring, when it is mild tasting but incredibly fragrant. If it's out of season, you can use baby spinach in this dish instead.

RISOTTO OF BROAD BEANS, WILD GARLIC & PARMESAN

Serves 2

Ingredients

750ml (1¼ pints) vegetable stock (see page 207)

1 tbsp olive oil

1 onion, peeled and diced

1 sprig of thyme

2 garlic cloves, peeled and crushed

1 bay leaf

350g (12oz) risotto rice

100ml (3½fl oz) white wine

75g (2½oz) unsalted butter

150g (5½oz) broad beans, cooked

4 wild garlic leaves, chopped

60g (2oz) Parmesan cheese, grated

Sea salt and cracked black pepper

1 Heat the vegetable stock and keep warm at the side of the stove until needed.

2 In a heavy saucepan, add the olive oil and then the onion, thyme, garlic and bay leaf and cook until the onion is translucent, but not coloured.

3 Add the rice and, using a wooden spoon, mix the rice into the onions. You should start to hear the rice crack. Once this happens, add the white wine followed by a ladleful of stock and begin to stir (the secret for a good risotto is lots of steam and lots of stirring). Make sure the rice has fully absorbed the stock before you add another ladle of stock. Continue adding stock until the rice is tender and cooked through.

4 Remove the pan from the heat and start to beat the butter into the rice. Add the broad beans and wild garlic leaves.

5 To serve, divide the risotto between 2 plates. Sprinkle over the grated Parmesan cheese and season with salt and pepper.

I like using Tagliatelle with this dish but you can really use any sort of pasta that you like. I always recommend that you try and get it fresh from a good delicatessen and it's also important to source really good fresh anchovies as you will notice such a difference in the taste.

TAGLIATELLE WITH CRISPY ANCHOVIES, LEMON, GARLIC, CHILLI & ROCKET

Serves 4

Ingredients

12 anchovy fillets

About 500ml (16fl oz) vegetable oil, for deep frying

Tempura batter (see page 208)

700g (1lb 9oz) fresh tagliatelle pasta

4 tbsp olive oil

2 garlic cloves, peeled and finely chopped

2 tbsp baby capers

2 small chillies, de-seeded and thinly sliced

Grated zest and juice of 2 lemons

100g (3½oz) rocket, chopped

50g (1¾oz) Parmesan cheese, grated

Cracked black pepper

1 Rinse the anchovy fillets under cold water and pat dry with kitchen paper.

2 Preheat the deep fat fryer to 190°C (375°F). Alternatively, half fill a deep saucepan with the vegetable oil and, using a cooking thermometer, heat to 190°C (375°F).

3 Dip the anchovy fillets into the tempura batter. Deep fry for 3 minutes or until lightly browned and crisp and then drain on kitchen paper.

4 Cook the tagliatelle in boiling salted water for 3 minutes.

5 While the pasta is cooking, heat the olive oil in a large saucepan over a high heat.

6 Add the garlic and capers and cook for 20 seconds.

7 Add the chillies, lemon juice and lemon rind and cook for a further minute. Season with pepper.

8 Drain the pasta and pour over the chilli mix. Add the rocket and stir thoroughly.

9 Divide the pasta evenly between 4 bowls, sprinkle over the Parmesan cheese and garnish with the crispy anchovy fillets.

DESSERTS

ALASTAIR
CHRISTIE
JERSEY
LAVENDER
FARM

The Jersey Lavender Farm is very much a family-run operation started by Alastair Christie's parents in 1983 when they converted the land and buildings from a derelict dairy farm.

Although it's a working farm, the Jersey Lavender Farm is very popular on the tourist trail as it's the only lavender farm in the Channel Islands.

I use lavender in a number of my recipes, some of which feature in this book. It's a versatile and wonderfully fragrant ingredient and, for me, the sight of the farm in full bloom, being busily farmed by bumblebees, is a quintessentially Jersey summer scene.

This is a quick and easy version of a classic French favourite. Serve it warm with crème fraîche or vanilla ice cream.

BAKED APPLE TART

Makes 6 individual tarts

Ingredients

Plain flour, for dusting

400g (14oz) ready-made puff pastry

6 apples

2 tbsp demerara sugar

Double cream, to serve

1 Preheat the oven to 200°C (400°F/Gas 6) and grease a baking tray.

2 Dust a flat surface with plain flour and roll out the puff pastry to approx 4mm (¼in) thick. Place on the baking tray and leave to rest in the fridge for 10 minutes.

3 Peel and core the apples and cut into quarters. Thinly slice the apples with a knife.

4 Remove the pastry from the fridge. Place a 15cm (6in) diameter saucer upside-down on the pastry and, with a sharp knife, cut around the saucer so you have a perfect circle. Cut out 6 circles from the pastry.

5 Arrange the apple slices in a circle around each tart.

6 Lightly sprinkle the apples with demerara sugar.

7 Transfer the tarts to baking trays and bake in the oven for 25 minutes.

8 Serve warm or at room temperature with a dollop of double cream.

These individual cheesecakes are a lovely treat. The compote can be used to dress a variety of other desserts.

BAKED VANILLA CHEESECAKE WITH BLACKBERRIES & MINT COMPOTE

Serves 6

Special equipment

Six 7.5–10cm (3–4in) diameter springform release tins

Ingredients

250g (9oz) blackberries

2 heaped tbsp icing sugar

Juice of ¼ lemon

110g (4oz) unsalted butter

225g (8oz) digestive biscuits

100ml (3½fl oz) double cream

2 eggs

175g (6oz) caster sugar

2 vanilla pods

675g (1½lb) cream cheese

6 mint leaves , chopped

1 To make the blackberry and mint compote, put the blackberries, icing sugar and lemon juice into a saucepan together with 3 tbsp of water. Bring to the boil and cook the fruit for 4 minutes. Transfer the blackberries and their juices to a bowl and leave to chill in the fridge.

2 For the cheesecakes, preheat the oven to 180°C (350°F/ Gas 4). Grease the base and sides of the individual tins.

3 Melt the butter in a saucepan and remove from the heat.

4 Place the biscuits in a plastic bag and crush with a rolling pin to make breadcrumbs. Mix thoroughly into the melted butter.

5 Place the biscuit mix into the cake tins so the coverage is about 1cm (½in) thick.

6 Using the back of a metal spoon, press down firmly and evenly on the biscuit until flat to form solid bases.

7 Place the cream, eggs and caster sugar into a large bowl and mix together well.

8 Split the vanilla pods and scrape the seeds into the mixture. Add in the cream cheese and beat until smooth.

9 Pour the mixture onto the biscuit bases. Bake in the oven for 30 minutes until set.

10 Turn the oven off and open the door, leaving the cheesecakes to bake out for 10 minutes before removing. Allow to cool.

11 Just before serving, add the mint leaves to the compote. Transfer the cheesecakes to plates and spoon over the blackberry compote.

This is my version of a great English classic. The moist almond filling is delicious with the homemade cherry jam.

CHERRY ALMOND TART

Serves 8

Special equipment

25cm (10in) loose-bottomed tart ring

Ingredients

For the cherry jam

750g (1lb 10oz) cherries, pitted

Juice of 2 lemons

Caster sugar (see method for details)

1 tbsp Kirsch

For the pastry

260g (9oz) plain flour

100g (3½oz) icing sugar

30g (1oz) ground almonds

125g (4½oz) unsalted butter, diced

1 egg

1 tsp milk

For the almond filling

25g (1oz) flaked almonds

125g (4½oz) unsalted butter, softened

125g (4½oz) caster sugar

3 eggs

150g (5½oz) ground almonds

Grated zest of 1 lemon

Preparation

1 Place the cherries in a heavy saucepan with 100ml (3½fl oz) water and the lemon juice. Bring to the boil, then reduce the heat to medium and cook for 20 minutes until soft.

2 Weigh the cherries. Whatever the weight of the cherries you will need to add three quarters of that weight again in sugar. For example, if you have 500g (1lb 2oz) of cooked cherries you will need 375g (13oz) of sugar).

3 Add the sugar and then place back into the saucepan.

4 Cook on a medium-high heat, stirring often with a wooden spoon, until the sugar has dissolved. Then continue to boil the jam for 10–15 minutes.

5 Once the jam starts to thicken, you can test it. Remove the jam from the heat and put a small spoonful onto a plate. Place in the fridge for 5 minutes until cold. If the jam has not set in this time, return the pan to the stove to continue cooking. Test every few minutes until the jam sets; be careful not to overcook the jam, as the sugar will caramelise.

6 Add the Kirsch and stir in well. This will bring back a fresh cherry flavour to the jam.

7 Cool and store in a sterilised jar with a lid until needed.

Method

1. To make the pastry, preheat the oven to 180°C (350°F/Gas 4).

2. In a large bowl, add the flour, sugar, almonds and diced butter. Using your fingertips, mix together until a crumb consistency is reached.

3. Add the eggs and mix well. Cover and leave to rest in the fridge for 30 minutes.

4. Roll out the pastry on a floured work surface to approx 2mm (⅛in) thick.

5. Line the tart ring with the pastry, letting it hang over the sides. Cover with cling film and fill the tart base with dry rice or baking beans.

6. Bake blind for about 20 minutes until cooked through and lightly golden. Remove the rice or baking beans and the cling film.

7. Mix the egg and milk in a small bowl. Using a pastry brush, egg wash the tart well and return to the oven for a further 3 minutes. Remove from the oven and set aside. Turn the oven down to 170°C (340°F /Gas 4).

8. For the almond filling, place the flaked almonds on a baking tray and toast them in the oven for 5 minutes. Put aside.

9. In a large bowl, cream the soft butter and caster sugar together and slowly stir in the eggs, a little at a time.

10. Fold in the ground almonds and beat well with a wooden spoon. Then beat in the lemon zest.

11. Spread cherry jam over the base of the cooked tart case. Spoon the almond filling on top. Using a wet palette knife, smooth off the top.

12. Sprinkle the toasted flaked almonds over the top and bake in the oven for 40 minutes. Allow to cool before removing from the tart tin and cutting into slices to serve.

The crunchy texture of the dried orange chips work really well with the smooth dark chocolate pudding.

DARK CHOCOLATE & ORANGE PUDDING

Serves 8

Special equipment

Food processor

1.7 litres (3 pints) deep-sided, oval, ovenproof dish

Electric whisk

Sugar thermometer

Ingredients

325g (11oz) caster sugar

3 oranges

1 star anise

125g (4½oz) ground almonds

4 whole eggs, plus 2 egg yolks

½ tsp baking powder

80g (3oz) granulated sugar

225g (8oz) good quality dark chocolate, plus shavings to decorate

250ml (8fl oz) whipping cream

Preparation

1 Preheat the oven to 100°C (210°F/lowest Gas).

2 Place 200g (7oz) of the caster sugar and 200ml (7fl oz) water in a saucepan and bring to the boil.

3 Slice 1 orange and add to the stock syrup.

4 Add the star anise and cook on a low heat for 20 minutes until the syrup is glossy and translucent. Allow to cool in the pan.

5 Lay the orange slices onto greaseproof paper and dry out in the oven for 3 hours. Break into small chips.

Method

1 For the orange sponge, preheat the oven to 180°C (350°F/Gas 4).

2 Boil the remaining 2 oranges whole in water for 30 minutes to take the bitterness out of the skin.

3 Cut the oranges in half, remove the pips and put in a food processor with the remaining 125g (4oz) caster sugar and the ground almonds, 3 eggs and baking powder. Blend until smooth.

4 Pour the mixture into the ovenproof dish and cook in the oven for 12–14 minutes, until golden brown. Allow to cool.

5 To make the topping, use an electric hand-held whisk to whisk together the remaining egg and 2 egg yolks in a large bowl, until they double in volume.

6 Bring the granulated sugar and 4 tsp of water to the boil and continue to boil until a sugar thermometer reads 'soft boil'. Remove the pan from the heat.

7 Add the sugar mixture to the eggs, whisking all the time.

8 Melt the dark chocolate in a bowl over hot water (or in a microwave), and pour into the egg mixture.

9 Whisk the cream until half whipped and then also fold into the chocolate mix.

10 Pour over the orange sponge and leave to set in the fridge for 2 hours.

11 Once set, top with the orange chips and shavings of dark chocolate.

A warm gooey brownie and the cold espresso are the perfect treat for any chocoholic.

DOUBLE CHOCOLATE & MACADAMIA NUT BROWNIES WITH ESPRESSO SHOTS

Makes 36 squares

Special equipment

23cm (9in) square baking tin

Ingredients

For the espresso shots

100ml (3½fl oz) double cream

4 tbsp coffee beans

70g (2½oz) good quality dark chocolate

3 tbsp coffee liqueur

For the chocolate brownies

80g (3oz) self-raising flour

300g (10oz) icing sugar

40g (1½oz) cocoa powder

300g (10oz) good quality dark chocolate

180g (6oz) unsalted butter

4 tsp golden syrup

2 vanilla pods

4 eggs

300g (10oz) white chocolate shavings or buttons

80g (2½oz) macadamia nuts

1 To make the espresso shots, place the cream and coffee beans in a saucepan and simmer on a low heat for 5 minutes. Remove from the heat and allow to infuse for 20 minutes.

2 Strain the cream into a clean pan and return to the stove.

3 Add the chocolate and stir until smooth before adding the coffee liqueur.

4 Pour into shot glasses and chill in the fridge until set.

5 For the chocolate brownies, preheat the oven to 180°C (350°F/Gas 4). Line the baking tin with baking parchment.

6 Sift the flour, icing sugar and cocoa powder into a bowl.

7 Place the chocolate, butter and golden syrup into a pan and melt. Scrape the insides of the vanilla pods into the mixture and stir to combine.

8 Carefully crack the eggs into a bowl and whisk, using an electric hand-held whisk if you have one.

9 Fold the warm melted chocolate mixture into the eggs.

10 Then fold in the flour mixture, making sure it is fully incorporated.

11 To finish, add the white chocolate and macadamia nuts. Pour the mixture into the baking tin and bake in the oven for 30 minutes.

12 When it's cool enough to handle, remove from the tray and cut into squares.

This is an ideal dessert to share with friends and family. I like to serve it with lashings of crème fraîche.

GLAZED LEMON TART

Serves 6–8

Special equipment

25cm (10in) deep flan tin
Dry rice or baking beans

Ingredients

260g (9oz) plain flour
100g (3½oz) icing sugar
40g (1½oz) ground almonds
125g (4½oz) unsalted butter, diced
5 eggs, plus 4 egg yolks
1 tsp milk
150g (6oz) caster sugar
Juice of 3½ lemons
225ml (7½fl oz) whipping cream

1 Preheat the oven to 180°C (340°F/Gas 4).

2 To make the pastry, put the flour, icing sugar, almonds and butter into a large mixing bowl. Using your fingertips, mix together into a crumb consistency.

3 Lightly beat 2 of the eggs and add most of it to the mixture and mix well. Cover the pastry and rest in the fridge for 30 minutes. Mix the remaining egg with the milk and set aside.

4 Lightly dust a work surface with flour. Roll out the pastry to about 2mm (⅛in) thick. Line the flan tin with the pastry, letting it hang over the sides.

5 Cover with cling film and fill the tart base with the rice or baking beans. Bake blind for about 20 minutes or until the case is cooked through and lightly golden.

6 Remove the baking beans and cling film. Using a pastry brush and the reserved egg and milk, egg wash the tart. Return it to the oven for a further 3 minutes. Remove from the oven, trim off any excess pastry and set aside. Reduce the oven temperature to 170°C (340°F/Gas 4).

7 To make the filling, mix together the caster sugar, egg yolks, remaining 3 eggs and lemon juice in a bowl.

8 Heat the cream in a small saucepan to boiling point then pour into the mixture. Mix well.

9 Pour the filling into the baked tart case and bake in the oven for 40 minutes. Leave to cool, then keep in the fridge until serving.

The warm roasted pears with fresh thyme work fantastically with the cold yogurt and spiced honey cake.

HONEY CAKE, ROASTED PEARS, YOGURT & HONEYCOMB

Serves 6

Special equipment

900g (2lb) loaf tin

Ingredients

200g (7oz) unsalted butter
130g (4½oz) dark soft brown sugar
300g (10oz) clear honey
280g (10oz) self-raising flour
½ tsp bicarbonate of soda
1 tsp cinnamon powder
2 tsp mixed spice powder
2 eggs
150ml (5fl oz) milk
4 pears
25g (1oz) caster sugar
75ml (2½fl oz) Poire William (sweet pear liqueur)
2 tsp thyme, plus sprigs to decorate
200g (7oz) natural yogurt
Fresh honeycomb, to serve

1 Preheat the oven to 180°C (350°F/Gas 4). Grease the loaf tin with butter and line with baking parchment.

2 Heat a saucepan and melt 175g (6oz) of the butter. Add the brown sugar and 250g (9oz) of honey and mix together.

3 Sift the flour and bicarbonate of soda into the butter mix.

4 Add the cinnamon and mixed spice and stir in well.

5 In a medium bowl beat the eggs with the milk then slowly beat into the rest of the mix.

6 Pour into the loaf tin and cook in the oven for 25–30 minutes. When the cake is cooked it will be golden brown, well-risen and firm when lightly pressed. Remove the cake from the oven.

7 Remove from the tin and leave on a wire cooling rack. Brush with the remainder of the honey and leave to cool.

8 Meanwhile, peel the pears, cut into quarters and remove the core and seeds with a small knife.

9 Place the pears in a dry hot pan. The pears will start to take on colour. When they start to turn golden brown, sprinkle the caster sugar into the pan.

10 When the sugar begins to caramelise, move them around in the pan to coat in the caramel. Add the Poire William and finish with the remaining 25g (1oz) of butter and the thyme.

11 To finish, take a slice of the honey cake, top with glazed pears and finish with a spoonful of natural yogurt. Sprinkle over more thyme and garnish with chunks of honeycomb.

ST SAMPSON, GUERNSEY

This is a really sociable dessert to share with friends or family. Place the lemon curd in the middle of the table and watch everyone tuck in.

LEMON CURD & DEEP-FRIED VANILLA SWEET DUMPLINGS

Serves 4

Ingredients

For the lemon curd

100g (3½oz) unsalted butter

Grated zest and juice of 2 lemons

225g (8oz) caster sugar

3 eggs, beaten

For the dumplings

120g (4oz) unsalted butter

85g (3oz) caster sugar

½ vanilla pod, split

Pinch of sea salt

500g (1lb 2oz) plain flour

2 eggs

½ x 15g packet of dried yeast

3 tbsp Poire William (sweet pear liqueur)

About 500ml (16fl oz) sunflower oil, for deep frying

Caster sugar, to dust

1 To make the lemon curd, melt the butter with the lemon zest in a large saucepan.

2 Mix the sugar, lemon juice and eggs in a large bowl.

3 Add the mixture to the melted butter and cook on a medium heat, stirring continuously until thickened.

4 Pass through a sieve into a fresh bowl and place in the fridge to cool.

5 To make the dumplings, warm 3 tbsp of water in a saucepan with the butter, caster sugar, vanilla pod and sea salt. Do not overheat.

6 Remove the vanilla pod and take the mixture off the heat.

7 Sift the flour into a mixing bowl.

8 In a separate mixing bowl, beat the eggs.

9 In another bowl, combine the yeast and the Poire William.

10 Add the eggs to the flour, then add the butter mixture and lastly the Poire William mix.

11 Combine to form a paste, cover with cling film and rest in the fridge.

12 When firm, roll out the dough to approximately 3mm (⅛in) on a floured surface.

13 Cut into strips 5cm (2in) long by 1cm (½in) wide.

14 Preheat the deep fat fryer to 170°C (340°F). Alternatively, half fill a deep saucepan with the sunflower oil and, using a cooking thermometer, heat to 170°C (340°F).

15 Fry the dumplings for 2 minutes or until golden brown. Remove from the oil and drain on kitchen paper.

16 Roll the sweet dumplings in sugar and serve warm with the lemon curd.

Lemon and raspberry is always a successful partnership. This is a really quick dessert to throw together for parties.

LEMON POSSET WITH RASPBERRIES

Serves 4

Special equipment

Pastry scraper

4 dessert glasses

Ingredients

600ml (1 pint) double cream

150g (5½oz) caster sugar

Juice of 3 lemons

250g (9oz) raspberries

100g (3½oz) white chocolate

1 Place the double cream and sugar into a large saucepan and bring to the boil.

2 Add the lemon juice to the saucepan, whisk well and remove from the heat.

3 Pour the mixture into a bowl and refrigerate to chill.

4 Divide the raspberries between the serving glasses.

5 Once the posset mixture is chilled, pour over the raspberries.

6 Leave to chill in the fridge for 30 minutes.

7 While the posset chills, make the white chocolate shavings.

8 Put the chocolate in a mixing bowl and melt in the microwave for 10 seconds at a time, stirring in between.

9 Pour the chocolate onto a clean work surface. When just set, use the pastry scraper at a 45-degree angle and push away from you into the chocolate to create shavings. Store them in a container in the freezer until needed.

10 Sprinkle the posset with the chocolate shavings and serve straight away.

This dish is fit for so many occasions from a sumptuous dinner with friends, to a family Sunday lunch, or even just with a good cuppa! It's so adaptable you can dress it up or leave it simple, but no matter how you serve it, it will always bring back childhood memories.

MY TREACLE TART WITH RASPBERRIES & CLOTTED CREAM

Serves 6–8

Special equipment

25cm (10in) loose-bottomed tart ring
Dry rice or baking beans

Ingredients

For the pastry

260g (9oz) plain flour
100g (3½oz) icing sugar
30g (1oz) ground almonds
125g (4½oz) unsalted butter, diced
3 eggs
1 tsp milk

1　Preheat the oven to 180°C (350°F/Gas 4).

2　To make the pastry, put the flour, sugar, almonds and butter in a large bowl. Using your fingertips, mix together into a crumb consistency.

3　Add 2 of the eggs and mix well. Cover and rest in the fridge for 30 minutes.

4　Lightly dust a work surface with flour. Roll out the pastry to about 2mm (⅛in) thick. Line the tart ring with the pastry, letting it hang over the sides.

5　Cover with cling film and fill the tart base with dry rice or baking beans. Bake blind for about 20 minutes or until the case is cooked through and lightly golden.

6　Remove the rice or baking beans and the cling film.

7　Mix the egg and milk in a small bowl. Using a pastry brush, egg wash the tart well and return to the oven for a further 3 minutes. Remove from the oven and set aside. Reduce the oven temperature to 160°C (325°F/Gas 3).

For the filling

60g (2oz) butter, unsalted
1 egg
1 egg yolk
3 tbsp double cream
6g salt
450g (1lb) golden syrup
120g (4oz) brown bread crumbs

To serve

250g (9oz) raspberries
½ lemon, juiced
1 tsp icing sugar
Cracked black pepper
Clotted cream

8   For the treacle tart filling, melt the butter in a saucepan until it starts to foam and turn brown, then take off the heat. Pour the butter through a sieve to remove the sediment.

9   Mix the egg, egg yolk, cream, and salt in a bowl.

10 In a saucepan heat the golden syrup gently for a few minutes until hot. Add the brown butter and mix well until it goes cloudy. Then add the cream mixture.

11 Add the breadcrumbs. Mix well and then pour the mixture into the cooked tart base.

12 Cook in the oven for 25 minutes and then reduce the temperature to 140°C (275°F/Gas 1) and cook for a further 20 minutes.

13 Remove from the oven and leave to cool for around 2 hours. The top should be chewy and the middle should be soft and moist with the pastry nice and crunchy.

14 When you are ready to serve, put the raspberries into a bowl and add the lemon juice and icing sugar. Mix well and finish with pepper to taste.

15 Cut the tart into portions and place on the plates. Scatter with the dressed raspberries and serve with the clotted cream.

Serving bread and butter pudding in blini pans is a great way to step this dish up for a dinner party. This is an old favourite with a modern twist.

ORANGE & LEMON BAKED BREAD & BUTTER PUDDING WITH MADEIRA SOAKED RAISINS

Serves 6

Special equipment

6 blini pans
(or individual ovenproof dishes)

Ingredients

100g (3½oz) golden raisins
4 tbsp Madeira wine
350ml (12fl oz) full-fat milk
3 tbsp double cream
2 eggs
4 tsp granulated sugar
12 slices white bread
50g (1¾oz) unsalted butter
6 tsp demerara sugar
Grated zest of 1 lemon
Grated zest of 1 orange

1 Preheat the oven to 170°C (340°F/Gas 4).

2 Place the raisins and Madeira wine in a saucepan. Boil off the Madeira wine for 8–10 minutes and then leave to cool.

3 To make the custard, gently warm the milk and cream in a pan over a low heat to scalding point. Don't let it boil.

4 Crack the eggs into a bowl, add the granulated sugar and lightly whisk until pale.

5 Add the warm milk and cream mixture and stir well, then strain the custard into a bowl. Cover with cling film to stop the custard from forming a skin and set aside.

6 Cut out 12 circles of white bread to the size of the blini pans.

7 Spread butter over the top of each round.

8 Sprinkle the bread with the demerara sugar.

9 Grease the blini pans with butter.

10 Place one piece of bread in the base of each pan and spoon half the raisins over the top.

11 Sprinkle with the grated lemon and orange rind.

12 Place the other circle of bread on top and spoon over the remaining raisins.

13 Pour the custard over and press down slightly so the bread absorbs the custard.

14 Bake in the oven for about 20 minutes, or until golden. Serve straight away.

189

We're lucky in Jersey to have a fantastic unique lavender farm. In summer months, when strawberries are in season, this makes a great dessert.

STRAWBERRY & LAVENDER PANNA COTTA WITH OLIVE OIL SHORTBREAD

Serves 6

Special equipment

6 dessert glasses

Ingredients

For the shortbread

115g (4oz) unsalted butter
100g (3½oz) caster sugar
200g (7oz) plain flour
50g (1¾oz) ground almonds
Pinch of salt
Pinch of baking powder
1 vanilla pod
2 large egg yolks
2 tbsp olive oil
Caster sugar, for dusting

1. To make the shortbread, mix together the butter and sugar in a large bowl.

2. Add the flour, ground almonds, salt and baking powder.

3. Split the vanilla pod down the middle lengthways and scrape out the seeds. Add a quarter of the seeds to the mixture.

4. Mix until it starts to combine. Then slowly add the egg yolks and olive oil.

5. Wrap the dough in cling film and place in the fridge for 1–2 hours.

6. When ready to cook the shortbread, preheat the oven to 180°C (350°F/Gas 4).

7. Roll out the dough onto greaseproof paper until 1cm (½in) thick. Carefully place onto a baking tray and cook in the oven for 10 minutes. Remove from the oven and cut into fingers.

8. Return to the oven and cook for a further 5–10 minutes.

9. Dust lightly with caster sugar, then allow to cool for 5 minutes before gently transferring them to a wire rack to cool completely.

For the panna cotta

10g sachet of gelatine

650ml (1 pint) whipping cream

120g (4½oz) caster sugar

10g (¼oz) dried lavender

500g (1lb 2oz) fresh strawberries

Black pepper

½ lemon

Icing sugar, to dust

10 To make the panna cotta, soak the gelatine in 90ml (3fl oz) of water.

11 Put the cream, caster sugar and lavender into a heavy saucepan and gently bring to the boil over a medium heat.

12 Add the gelatine water. Stir and then pass through a fine sieve into a jug.

13 Blend 250g (9oz) of strawberries in a liquidiser and add to the mix, blend well.

14 Cut the remaining strawberries in half, mix with some black pepper, a squeeze of lemon juice and a dusting of icing sugar.

15 Place a spoonful of strawberries in the bottom of each glass. Pour over the panna cotta mix dividing evenly between the glasses.

16 Place in the fridge for 1 hour until set.

17 Serve with a couple of fingers of shortbread.

193

BREADS

CHORIZO &
PARMESAN FOCACCIA

Makes 490g (1lb 2oz)

Special equipment

Electric mixer

Ingredients

50g (1¾oz) chorizo, skinned

2 tbsp olive oil

375g (13oz) white strong flour

50g (1¾oz) Parmesan cheese, grated

2 tsp sea salt

1   Slowly fry the chorizo in the olive oil. Once browned, finely dice the chorizo and leave in the oil until cold enough to use for the bread.

2   In an electric mixer add the flour, chorizo, 2 tbsp of the chorizo oil, Parmesan and 200ml (7fl oz) of water. Using a dough hook, mix on a medium speed for 6 minutes.

3   Add the salt and mix for a further 6 minutes.

4   Cover with a damp cloth and leave it to prove for 1 hour in a warm area.

5   Place the dough on a lightly floured surface and, with the palm of your hand, knock the dough back.

6   Next, roll and shape the dough.

7   Rest for a further 20 minutes. Preheat the oven to 180°C (350°F/Gas 4).

8   Brush the top with more chorizo oil before baking in the oven for 15–20 minutes or until cooked. Check by tapping the base of the bread with your fingers; if it sounds hollow, it's ready.

9   Remove from the oven and leave to cool.

OLIVE BREAD

Makes 360g (12oz)

Special equipment

Electric mixer

Ingredients

250g (9oz) strong plain flour

1 tsp salt

12g (½oz) fresh yeast

60g (2oz) green olives, pitted

2 tbsp olive oil

1 Preheat the oven to 180°C (350°F/Gas 4).

2 Place the flour, salt and yeast into the bowl of the mixer and, using a dough hook, mix for 2 minutes on a slow speed.

3 Add the olives, 2 tsp of water and the olive oil and mix on half speed for 3 minutes.

4 Remove the bowl from the machine and place a damp, clean cloth over the top. Set aside in a warm area and leave to rise for 35 minutes or until doubled in volume.

5 Remove the dough from the bowl onto a clean work surface. Using the palm of your hand knock the dough back.

6 Place the dough back into the bowl, leave for 35 minutes and repeat the same process.

7 After the second knock back, roll and shape the dough and place onto a baking tray, cover, and prove in a warm environment for 30 minutes or until you can see that it has doubled in size.

8 Bake in the oven for 35 minutes or until cooked. Check by tapping the base of the bread with your fingers; if it sounds hollow, it's ready.

9 Remove from the oven and leave to cool.

SUN-DRIED TOMATO BREAD

Makes 330g (11oz)

Special equipment

Electric mixer

Ingredients

250g (9oz) strong plain flour

1 tsp table salt

½ x 15g packet of dried yeast

50g (1¾oz) sun-dried tomatoes

1 tbsp sun-dried tomato oil

1 Place the flour, salt and yeast into the mixer. Using a dough hook, start the mixer on a slow speed and mix for 2 minutes. Add 110ml (4 fl oz) of room temperature water followed by the sun-dried tomatoes and the oil. Mix on a medium speed for 4 minutes.

2 Cover with a clean, damp cloth and leave in a warm area for 25 minutes.

3 When the dough has doubled in volume, remove from the bowl and place on the work surface. Using the palm of your hand knock the dough back.

4 Place the dough back into the bowl and cover, repeat the same process after a further 25 minutes.

5 Preheat the oven to 180°C (350°F/Gas 4).

6 After the second knock back, shape the dough into a round ball and place onto a floured tray and leave until it doubles in size.

7 Sift a small amount of flour onto the dough before placing in the oven.

8 Bake in the oven for 35 minutes, or until cooked. Check by tapping the base of the bread with your fingers; if it sounds hollow, it's ready.

9 Remove from the oven and leave to cool.

SUNFLOWER SEED BREAD

Makes 295g (10oz)

Special equipment

Electric mixer

Ingredients

250g (9oz) granary flour

1 tsp salt

12g (½oz) fresh yeast

25g (1oz) sunflower seeds

1 Place all the dry ingredients into an electric mixer, making sure the salt does not touch the yeast. Use a dough hook and dry mix for 30 seconds.

2 Slowly add 140ml (5fl oz) of water and mix on speed 1 for 3 minutes.

3 Mix for a further 5 minutes on speed 2 adding another 3 tbsp of water in 2 stages.

4 Cover with a damp cloth for 30 minutes to prove.

5 Remove the dough from the bowl onto a lightly floured work surface and with palm of your hand knock the dough back. Place back into the bowl and cover.

6 Leave for a further 30 minutes and then repeat the same process.

7 After 15 minutes, remove from the bowl onto a lightly floured work surface, cover with cling film and leave for 10 minutes.

8 Next roll and shape the dough.

9 Finally, dip the bread dough face down onto the sunflower seeds.

10 Preheat the oven to 210°C (400°F/Gas 6).

11 Place the dough onto a baking tray, cover, and prove in a warm environment for 30 minutes or until you can see that it has doubled in size.

12 Bake in the oven for 25 minutes or until cooked. Check by tapping the base of the bread with your fingers; if it sounds hollow, it's ready.

13 Remove from the oven and leave to cool.

PANTRY

BRIOCHE

Ingredients

500g (1lb 2oz) plain flour

6 eggs

50g (1¾oz) sugar

2 tsp salt

50g (1¾oz) fresh yeast

250g (9oz) butter, diced

1 Preheat the oven to 180°C (350°F/Gas 4).

2 Put the flour, eggs, sugar and salt into a mixing bowl and mix for 5 minutes.

3 Add the yeast and then mix for a further 5 minutes.

4 Add the diced butter and mix until the dough is shiny and stretchy.

5 Grease small brioche moulds with oil and place 40g (1½oz) of dough in each one.

6 Leave to prove in a warm area for 25 minutes.

7 Bake in the oven for 8 minutes.

BEARNAISE SAUCE

Ingredients

3 tbsp tarragon vinegar

100ml (3½fl oz) white wine

4 black peppercorns, crushed

2 shallots, peeled and sliced

4 sprigs of tarragon

1 bay leaf

3 egg yolks

250g (9oz) warm clarified butter (see page 50)

Sea salt and cracked black pepper

Juice of ¼ lemon

1 Place the vinegar, white wine, crushed peppercorns, shallots, tarragon stalks (reserve the leaves) and bay leaf into a saucepan. Reduce until you have 2 tbsp of liquid left, remove from the stove and allow to cool, then strain.

2 Half fill a saucepan with water and bring to the boil.

3 Put the egg yolks and vinegar reduction into a mixing bowl, place it on top of the boiling water and start to whisk the eggs. Remove the bowl every 10 seconds to prevent the eggs from scrambling. Continue to whisk the yolks until they have doubled in volume and become very light.

4 Pour the warm clarified butter into the sauce little by little; if you add it too fast, the sauce will split. If you think the mix is getting too thick, add 1 tsp of hot water. Let it cool down and then carry on whisking the butter until it is all incorporated.

5 Chop the tarragon leaves. Season the sauce with salt and pepper, then add the chopped tarragon leaves and the lemon juice.

TARTARE SAUCE

Ingredients

3 egg yolks
1 tbsp Dijon mustard
1 tbsp white wine vinegar
500ml (16fl oz) olive oil
Salt and cracked black pepper
Juice of ½ lemon
3 tbsp baby capers
3 tbsp diced cornichons
3 tbsp diced shallots
1 tbsp chopped flat-leaf parsley

1 In a food processer blend the egg yolks, mustard and vinegar until smooth.

2 Slowly add the olive oil to the eggs, taking care not to let the mixture separate. If it looks like it's going to split, add 1 tsp of cold water.

3 Season with salt and pepper and add the lemon juice.

4 To finish, add the baby capers, cornichons, shallots and parsley and mix well.

5 Store in the fridge until needed.

AIOLI

Ingredients

1 pinch of saffron
3 garlic cloves, peeled and finely chopped
2 egg yolks
50g (1¾oz) mashed potato
140ml (5fl oz) olive oil (best quality available)
Sea salt and cracked black pepper

1 Put the saffron, garlic, egg yolks and mashed potato into a food processor, or blender, and blend until the mix is thick and smooth.

2 While continuing to blend, slowly pour in the olive oil and mix until fully combined.

3 Season with salt and pepper to taste and finish blending.

4 Pour the mixture into a jar/container with a re-sealable lid and store in the fridge

MADEIRA SAUCE

Ingredients

2 tbsp olive oil
6 shallots, peeled and finely chopped
½ garlic bulb, peeled and chopped
3 sprigs of thyme
1 bay leaf
750ml (1¼ pints) Madeira wine
10 button mushrooms, sliced
1 litre (1¾pints) chicken stock (see page 207), reduced
2 tomatoes, halved and seeds removed
2 sprigs of tarragon

1 Heat the olive oil in a large saucepan over a medium heat.

2 Add the shallots, garlic, thyme and bay leaf to the pan and sauté for about 2 minutes, or until the shallots are soft.

3 Add the Madeira wine to the pan along with the sliced mushrooms. Bring to the boil and reduce the Madeira by two thirds.

4 Next, add the chicken stock, tomatoes and fresh tarragon. Bring back to the boil and simmer for 15 minutes.

5 Remove from the heat and skim the fat and impurities off the surface with a ladle.

6 Pass the sauce through a sieve into a suitable container. Once cooled, store in the fridge.

MAYONNAISE

Ingredients

3 egg yolks

1 tbsp Dijon mustard

1 tbsp white wine vinegar

500ml (16fl oz) olive oil

Salt and cracked black pepper

Juice of ½ lemon

1 In a food processer blend the egg yolks, mustard and vinegar until smooth.

2 Whilst continuing to blend, slowly pour in the olive oil and mix until fully combined. If it looks like the mixture is going to split, add 1 tsp of cold water.

3 Season with salt and pepper and add the lemon juice.

4 Store in the fridge until needed.

TARAMOSALATA

Ingredients

125g (4½oz) smoked cod roe

1 garlic clove, peeled and crushed

2 tsp Dijon mustard

1 tsp salt

50g (1¾oz) white breadcrumbs, soaked in milk

225ml (8fl oz) grape seed oil

3 tbsp extra virgin olive oil

Juice of 1 lemon

White pepper

1 Place the cod roe, garlic, mustard, salt and 3 tbsp of water in a food processor and blend until smooth.

2 Drain the breadcrumbs and add to the food processor. Continue to blend the mixture.

3 While blending, slowly add the grape seed oil, followed by the olive oil.

4 Add the lemon juice and season with white pepper.

5 Pour the mixture into a bowl, cover with cling film and place in the fridge until needed.

HUMMUS

Ingredients

2 x 400g tins cooked chickpeas

125ml (4½fl oz) olive oil

200ml (7fl oz) vegetable oil

100ml (3½fl oz) lemon juice

3 garlic cloves, peeled and crushed

2 tsp smoked paprika, plus extra for serving

170g (6oz) tahini paste

Sea salt and cracked white pepper

1 Drain the chickpeas and rinse thoroughly.

2 In a saucepan, warm the olive oil and the vegetable oil over a low heat. Keep warm.

3 Pour the chickpeas into a food processor. Add the lemon juice, garlic, smoked paprika and tahini paste. Blend until smooth.

4 Slowly pour in the oils. If the hummus starts to get too thick, add some water. Season with salt and white pepper.

5 To serve, spoon into a bowl, drizzle with a little olive oil and dust lightly with smoked paprika.

CHICKEN STOCK

Ingredients

4 chicken carcases

1 large onion, peeled and halved

1 large carrot, peeled and halved

1 celery stick

1 leek, trimmed and halved

1 Place the chicken bones in a large saucepan and cover with cold water.

2 Bring to the boil and take all the scum off the surface.

3 Reduce the heat to a simmer and then add all the vegetables. Leave to simmer for 3–4 hours.

4 Strain the liquid into a clean bowl and leave to cool. Keep in the fridge or freezer until needed.

5 If concentrated chicken stock is required, then return to the pan and again reduce by half.

FISH STOCK

Ingredients

20g (1oz) unsalted butter

1 celery stick, roughly chopped

2 onions, peeled and roughly chopped

1 leek, trimmed and roughly chopped

I bay leaf

1 stalk lemongrass

6 coriander seeds

1 star anise

6 white peppercorns

100ml (3½fl oz) white wine

1kg (2¼lb) white fish bones

3 parsley stalks

1 In a large saucepan over a low heat, gently warm the butter. Then add the celery, onion, leek, bay leaf, lemongrass, coriander seeds, star anise and white peppercorns. Cook until soft.

2 Add the white wine and reduce until all of the wine has evaporated.

3 Add the fish bones and parsley stalks to the pan. Pour in enough cold water to cover the contents and bring to the boil.

4 Skim the surface and remove any impurities. Turn down the heat and simmer for about 20 minutes.

5 Remove the pan from the heat and set aside to allow the stock to settle before straining off through a sieve into a suitable container.

6 Store in a sealed container in the fridge or freezer until needed.

VEGETABLE STOCK

Ingredients

3 large onions, peeled and diced

3 large carrots, peeled and diced

2 celery sticks, diced

2 leeks, trimmed and sliced

6 black peppercorns, crushed

1 tsp coriander seeds

2 bay leaves

1 star anise

2 parsley stalks (optional)

1 Place all the ingredients into a saucepan. Cover with 2 litres (3½ pints) of cold water and bring to the boil.

2 Leave to simmer and reduce for 25 minutes and then take off the heat.

3 Leave to stand for 15 minutes then strain the liquid into a clean bowl and leave to cool.

4 Store in the fridge or freezer until needed.

ONION & THYME SCENTED GRAVY

Ingredients

1 tbsp olive oil

50g (1¾oz) butter, unsalted

4 onions, peeled and sliced

4 sprigs of thyme

2 garlic cloves, peeled

100ml (3½fl oz) white wine

1 litre (1¾ pints) chicken stock (see page 207)

1 Heat the olive oil and butter in a large saucepan. Add the onions, thyme and garlic and cook until the onions become soft and translucent.

2 Add the white wine and chicken stock and bring up to the boil.

3 Turn down the heat and simmer for 30 minutes.

TEMPURA BATTER

Ingredients

Generous tablespoon of cornflour

90g (3oz) plain flour

Pinch of bicarbonate of soda

Pinch of sea salt

240ml (8fl oz) carbonated mineral water

1 Sift all of the dry ingredients into a mixing bowl.

2 Whisk in the mineral water making sure there are no lumps.

3 Cover and store in the fridge until needed.

KUMQUAT CHUTNEY

Ingredients

300g (10oz) kumquats, halved

1 vanilla pod, split in half

1 star anise

6 coriander seeds

1 cinnamon stick

Grated zest and juice of 2 oranges

150g (5½oz) granulated sugar

1 bay leaf

3½ tbsp Cointreau

Juice of ½ lemon

1 Place all the ingredients in a large saucepan with 150ml (5fl oz) water.

2 Bring to the boil and simmer until the skins of the kumquats are soft.

3 Remove from the heat and strain all the ingredients through a sieve into a large bowl. Set the liquid aside.

4 Remove the kumquats left in the sieve and scrape out their pulp.

5 Pass the pulp through the sieve into the reserved cooking liquid.

6 Next add the kumquat skins to the liquid and mix together well.

7 Pour the liquid into an airtight container and store in the fridge.

MY VINAIGRETTE

Ingredients

1 small shallot, trimmed and finely chopped

1 small garlic clove, peeled and finely chopped

1 tsp Dijon mustard

3 tbsp sherry vinegar

125ml (4fl oz) olive oil

125ml (4fl oz) vegetable oil

125ml (4fl oz) walnut oil

Salt and cracked black pepper

1 Put all the ingredients into a large glass jar or bottle, with a good fitting lid.

2 Season with salt and pepper. Give the jar a good shake and taste to check the seasoning.

3 Store in the fridge, shake well before use.

MUSHROOMS A LA GRECQUE

Ingredients

500ml (16fl oz) olive oil

25g (1oz) coriander seeds

5 shallots, trimmed and sliced

2kg (4½lbs) shiitake mushrooms, cleaned

Handful of rosemary, chopped

Handful of thyme, chopped

5 garlic cloves, peeled and sliced

1 Place the olive oil, coriander seeds, shallots and 1 litre (1¾ pints) of water in a saucepan and bring to a simmer.

2 Place the mushrooms in the liquid, remove from the heat and allow to cool.

3 Add the chopped rosemary and thyme and then the sliced garlic.

4 Leave to infuse, storing in a sterilised jar with a tight fitting lid.

5 Use straight from the jar with hot meats, salads and aperitifs.

SWEET PICKLED DUCK EGGS

Ingredients

570ml (1 pint) distilled vinegar

400g (14oz) caster sugar

2 star anise

2 kaffir lime leaves

2 tsp peeled and sliced fresh ginger

6 duck eggs

1 Place the vinegar and sugar in a heavy saucepan with 570ml (1 pint) water and bring to the boil. Simmer until the sugar has dissolved and then set aside to cool until needed.

2 While cooling, add the star anise, lime leaves and sliced ginger. Put aside.

3 Cook the duck eggs in salted boiling water for 15 minutes and then refresh the eggs by running them under cold water. Once cold, peel and wash the eggs and place them in the cold pickling liquid.

4 Store In a clean sterilised jar with a tight fitting lid until needed.

SHAUN & DON THOMPSON, LES ECREHOUS

INDEX

A

Aioli

Aioli 205

Grilled red mullet with roast provençal vegetables & aioli 88

Almond

Cherry almond tart 170

American-style pancakes with honey, Greek yogurt & pecan nuts 14

Anchovies

Pan-roasted lamb leg chops with caper, parsley, mint & anchovy butter 118

Tagliatelle with crispy anchovies, lemon, garlic, chilli & rocket 160

Apple

Apple & cinnamon muffins 16

Baked apple tart 166

Cheese soufflé with apple, walnut & pomegranate salad 150

Chicken liver parfait with apple & quince purée & warm toasted brioche 34

Roast rack of pork with baked apples & soft Parmesan polenta 126

Asparagus

Asparagus, roast red onion & Fort Grey cheese tarts 148

Crispy poached duck eggs with griddled asparagus 36

Sea trout with asparagus & pink grapefruit sabayon 104

Sea bass poached in confit lemon butter with asparagus & Royal Bay oysters 102

Avocado

Roast scallops with avocado, French beans & hazelnut dressing 48

B

Baked apple tart 166

Baked vanilla cheesecake with blackberries & mint compote 168

Basil

Cockles cooked in white wine with shallots, pancetta & basil 80

Slow-cooked lamb shank, spring vegetables & basil broth 136

Sweetcorn & basil soup with crispy tempura crab claws 74

Batter

Tempura batter 208

Béarnaise sauce 204

Beef

Carpaccio of fillet with a horseradish bavoire & woodland mushroom salad 32

The perfect Sunday roast 140

Blackberries

Baked vanilla cheesecake with blackberries & mint compote 168

Black pudding

Grilled black pudding with fried hen's eggs, forestière garnish & watercress 22

Breads

Brioche 204

Chorizo & Parmesan focaccia 194

Olive bread 196

Sun-dried tomato bread 198

Sunflower seed bread 200

BREAKFAST & BRUNCH

American-style pancakes with honey, Greek yogurt & pecan nuts 14

Apple & cinnamon muffins 16

French toast with smoked bacon, maple syrup & rocket salad 18

Grilled black pudding with fried hen's eggs, forestière garnish & watercress 22

Warm potato pancake with smoked salmon & scrambled eggs 24

Welsh rarebit with cured bacon 26

Brioche 204

Broad beans

Herb gnocchi with broad beans & Pecorino 152

Risotto of broad beans, wild garlic & Parmesan 158

Broccoli

Tender-stem broccoli with garlic 143

C

Carrots

Roast carrots with rosemary & cardamom 143

Cheese

Baked vanilla cheesecake with blackberries & mint compote 168

Cheese soufflé with apple, walnut & pomegranate salad 150

Chorizo & Parmesan focaccia 194

French onion soup with thyme & Beaufort cheese croutes 64

Herb gnocchi with broad beans & Pecorino 152

Risotto of broad beans, wild garlic & Parmesan 158

Roast Jersey Royals with glazed pear, Roquefort cheese & walnut salad 44

Roast rack of pork with baked apples & soft Parmesan polenta 126

Cherry

Cherry almond tart 170

Chicken

Chicken, leek & mushroom plate pie 112

Chicken liver parfait with apple & quince purée & warm toasted brioche 34

Chicken & potato soup with scallops, chorizo & chicken scratching 60

Chicken stock 207

Sweet chilli chicken with garlic, lemon & coriander 52

Chilled watercress soup with dressed Asian pear & garden peas 62

Chips

Roasted lobster, triple-cooked chips & béarnaise sauce 98

Chorizo & Parmesan focaccia 194

Chocolate

Dark chocolate & orange pudding 172

Double chocolate & macadamia nut brownies with espresso shots 174

Chorizo

Chorizo & Parmesan focaccia 194

Linguine with mussels, chorizo, tomato & herb vierge 156

Cockles

Cockles cooked in white wine with shallots, Pancetta & basil 80

Coffee

Double chocolate & macadamia nut brownies with espresso shots 174

Confit of duck legs with vanilla & spiced kumquat chutney 114

Courgettes

Minestrone soup with baby courgettes 70

Crab

Dressed crab with spring onions, toasted sweetcorn, red chilli & coriander 84

Sweetcorn & basil soup with crispy tempura crab claws 74

Crispy poached duck eggs with griddled asparagus 36

Crispy whiting fingers in lemonade batter with minted peas 82

Cucumber

Fresh oysters with three dressings: cucumber pickle, shallot & red wine vinegar, gin & tonic mint jelly 41

Smoked salmon terrine with cucumber salad & soft quail's eggs 50

Curried scallops with coconut & coriander dahl & apple salad 38

D

Dark chocolate & orange pudding 172

Dates

Roast venison loin with parsnips, cardamom-scented quinoa & medjool dates 128

DESSERTS

Apple & cinnamon muffins 16

Baked apple tart 166

Baked vanilla cheesecake with blackberries & mint compote 168

Cherry almond tart 170

Dark chocolate & orange pudding 172

Double chocolate & macadamia nut brownies with espresso shots 174

Glazed lemon tart 176

Honey cake, roasted pears, yogurt & honeycomb 178

Lemon curd & deep-fried vanilla sweet dumplings 182

Lemon posset with raspberries 184

My treacle tart with raspberries & clotted cream 186

Orange & lemon baked bread & butter pudding with Madeira soaked raisins 188

Strawberry & lavender panna cotta with olive oil shortbread 190

Dips

Hummus 206

Taramosalata 206

Double chocolate & macadamia nut brownies with espresso shots 174

Dover sole

Grilled Dover sole with garden peas & crispy pancetta salad 86

Dressed crab with spring onions, toasted sweetcorn, red chilli & coriander 84

Duck

Confit of duck legs with vanilla & spiced kumquat chutney 114

Duck eggs

Crispy poached duck eggs with griddled asparagus 36

Sweet pickled duck eggs 209

E

F

Fennel

Lobster salad with marinated fennel & chunky spicy guacamole 90

FISH

Crispy whiting fingers in lemonade batter with minted peas 82

Gazpacho soup with grilled sardines on toast 68

Grilled Dover sole with garden peas & crispy pancetta salad 86

Grilled red mullet with roast Provençal vegetables & aioli 88

Mackerel with English salad & orange, lemon & grain mustard dressing 94

Sea bass en papillote in Asian aromats 100

Sea bass poached in confit lemon butter with asparagus & Royal Bay oysters **102**

Sea trout with asparagus & pink grapefruit sabayon **104**

Smoked salmon terrine with cucumber salad & soft quail's eggs **50**

Tagliatelle with crispy anchovies, lemon, garlic, chilli & rocket **160**

Taramosalata **206**

Traunch of turbot with a smoked salmon, horseradish & spring pea salad **106**

Warm potato pancake with smoked salmon & scrambled eggs **24**

Yellow fin tuna with lime & white radish dressing & Bloody Mary jelly **54**

Fish stock **207**

Focaccia

Chorizo & Parmesan focaccia **194**

French beans

Roast scallops with avocado, French beans & hazelnut dressing **48**

French onion soup with thyme & Beaufort cheese croutes **64**

French toast with smoked bacon, maple syrup & rocket salad **18**

Fresh oysters with three dressings: cucumber pickle, shallot & red wine vinegar, gin & tonic mint jelly **41**

G

GAME

Roast pheasant with orange & onion marmalade & juices **120**

Roast rabbit loin in pancetta with Moroccan-style couscous & calamari **122**

Roast venison loin with parsnips, cardamom-scented quinoa & medjool dates **128**

Gazpacho

Gazpacho soup with grilled sardines on toast **68**

Glazed lemon tart **176**

Gnocchi

Herb gnocchi with broad beans & Pecorino **152**

Grapefruit

Sea trout with asparagus & pink grapefruit sabayon **104**

Grilled black pudding with fried hen's eggs, forestière garnish & watercress **22**

Grilled Dover sole with garden peas & crispy pancetta salad **86**

Grilled red mullet with roast Provençal vegetables & aioli **88**

Guacamole

Lobster salad with marinated fennel & chunky spicy guacamole **90**

H

Hen's eggs

Grilled black pudding with fried hen's eggs, forestière garnish & watercress **22**

Warm potato pancake with smoked salmon & scrambled eggs **24**

Herb gnocchi with broad beans & Pecorino **152**

Honey

American-style pancakes with honey, Greek yogurt & pecan nuts **14**

Honey cake, roasted pears, yogurt & honeycomb **178**

Slow-cooked belly pork glazed with honey & grain mustard **132**

Horseradish

Carpaccio of fillet with a horseradish bavoire & woodland mushroom salad **32**

Hummus **206**

I

J

Jersey Royals

Roast Jersey Royal salad with maple syrup, confit garlic, red onion & crispy pancetta **42**

Roast Jersey Royals with glazed pear, Roquefort cheese & walnut salad **44**

K

Kumquat

Confit of duck legs with vanilla & spiced kumquat chutney **114**

Kumquat chutney **208**

L

Lamb

Pan-roasted lamb leg chops with caper, parsley, mint & anchovy butter **118**

Shoulder of lamb cooked in hay with lavender, herbs & garlic **130**

Slow-cooked lamb shank, spring vegetables & basil broth **136**

LARDER

Aioli **205**

Béarnaise sauce **204**

Brioche **204**

Chicken stock **207**

Fish stock **207**

Hummus **206**

Kumquat chutney **208**

Madeira sauce **205**

Mayonnaise **206**

Mushrooms à la grecque **209**

Onion & thyme scented gravy **208**

Sweet pickled duck eggs **209**

Taramosalata **206**

Tartare sauce **205**

Tempura batter **208**

Vegetable stock **207**

My Vinaigrette **209**

Lavender

Shoulder of lamb cooked in hay with lavender, herbs & garlic 130

Strawberry & lavender panna cotta with olive oil shortbread 190

Leek

Chicken, leek & mushroom plate pie 112

Lemon

Glazed lemon tart 176

Lemon curd & deep-fried vanilla sweet dumplings 182

Lemon posset with raspberries 184

Orange & lemon baked bread & butter pudding with Madeira soaked raisins 188

Sea bass poached in confit lemon butter with asparagus & Royal Bay oysters 102

Linguine

Linguine with mussels, chorizo, tomato & herb vierge 156

Lobster

Lobster salad with marinated fennel & chunky spicy guacamole 90

Roasted Lobster, triple-cooked chips & béarnaise sauce 98

M

Macadamia nuts

Double chocolate & macadamia nut brownies with espresso shots 174

Mackerel

Mackerel with English salad & orange, lemon & grain mustard dressing 94

Madeira

Madeira sauce 205

Orange & lemon baked bread & butter pudding with Madeira soaked raisins 188

Mayonnaise 206

MEAT

Carpaccio of fillet with a horseradish bavoire & woodland mushroom salad 32

French toast with smoked bacon, maple syrup & rocket salad 18

Grilled black pudding with fried hen's eggs, forestière garnish & watercress 22

My mum's ham hock, split yellow pea & barley soup 72

Pan-roasted lamb leg chops with caper, parsley, mint & anchovy butter 118

Roast rack of pork with baked apples & soft Parmesan polenta 126

Shoulder of lamb cooked in hay with lavender, herbs & garlic 130

Slow-cooked belly pork glazed with honey & grain mustard 132

Slow-cooked lamb shank, spring vegetables & basil broth 136

Sweet chilli chicken with garlic, lemon & coriander 52

The perfect Sunday roast 140

Welsh rarebit with cured bacon 26

Yorkshire pudding with onion gravy 141

Minestrone soup with baby courgettes 70

Mint

Baked vanilla cheesecake with blackberries & mint compote 168

Muffins

Apple & cinnamon muffins 16

Mushrooms

Carpaccio of fillet with a horseradish bavoire & woodland mushroom salad 32

Chicken, leek & mushroom plate pie 112

Grilled black pudding with fried hen's eggs, forestière garnish & watercress 22

Mushrooms à la grecque 209

Mussels

Linguine with mussels, chorizo, tomato & herb vierge 156

Mustard

Mackerel with English salad & orange, lemon & grain mustard dressing 94

Slow-cooked belly pork glazed with honey & grain mustard 132

My coq au vin 116

My mum's ham hock, split yellow pea & barley soup 72

My treacle tart with raspberries & clotted cream 186

N

O

Olives

Olive bread 196

Onion

Asparagus, roast red onion & Fort Grey cheese tarts 148

French onion soup with thyme & Beaufort cheese croutes 64

Onion & thyme scented gravy 208

Roast Jersey Royal salad with maple syrup, confit garlic, red onion & crispy pancetta 42

Roast pheasant with orange & onion marmalade & juices 120

Roast red onions in their skins 143

Yorkshire pudding with onion gravy 141

Orange

Dark chocolate & orange pudding 172

Mackerel with English salad & orange, lemon & grain mustard dressing 94

Orange & lemon baked bread & butter pudding with Madeira soaked raisins 188

Roast pheasant with orange & onion marmalade & juices 120

Oysters

Fresh oysters with three dressings: cucumber pickle, shallot & red wine vinegar, gin & tonic mint jelly 41

Sea bass poached in confit lemon butter with asparagus & Royal Bay oysters 102

P

Pancakes

American-style pancakes with honey, Greek yogurt & pecan nuts 14

Pancetta

Cockles cooked in white wine with shallots, pancetta & basil 80

Roast Jersey Royal salad with maple syrup, confit garlic, red onion & crispy pancetta 42

Roast rabbit loin in pancetta with Moroccan-style couscous & calamari 122

Panna cotta

Strawberry & lavender panna cotta with olive oil shortbread 190

Pan-roasted lamb leg chops with caper, parsley, mint & anchovy butter 118

PASTA

Linguine with mussels, chorizo, tomato & herb vierge 156

Tagliatelle with crispy anchovies, lemon, garlic, chilli & rocket 160

Pear

Chilled watercress soup with dressed Asian pear & garden peas 62

Honey cake, roasted pears, yogurt & honeycomb 178

The perfect Sunday roast 140

Pheasant

Roast pheasant with orange & onion marmalade & juices 120

Pomegranate

Cheese soufflé with apple, walnut & pomegranate salad 150

Pork

Roast rack of pork with baked apples & soft Parmesan polenta 126

Slow-cooked belly pork glazed with honey & grain mustard 132

My mum's ham hock, split yellow pea & barley soup 72

Potato

Chicken & potato soup with scallops, chorizo & chicken scratching 60

Roast potatoes with thyme 142

Warm potato pancake with smoked salmon & scrambled eggs 24

POULTRY

Chicken, leek & mushroom plate pie 112

Chicken liver parfait with apple & quince purée & warm toasted brioche 34

Chicken & potato soup with scallops, chorizo & chicken scratching 60

Confit of duck legs with vanilla & spiced kumquat chutney 114

My coq au vin 116

Quince

Chicken liver parfait with apple & quince purée & warm toasted brioche 34

Quinoa

Roast venison loin with parsnips, cardamom-scented quinoa & medjool dates 128

Rabbit

Roast rabbit loin in pancetta with Moroccan-style couscous & calamari 122

Radish

Yellow fin tuna with lime & white radish dressing & Bloody Mary jelly 54

Rarebit

Welsh rarebit with cured bacon 26

Raspberries

My treacle tart with raspberries & clotted cream 186

Red mullet

Grilled red mullet with roast Provençal vegetables & aioli 88

Risotto

Risotto of broad beans, wild garlic & Parmesan 158

Risotto of shellfish 96

Roast carrots with rosemary & cardamom 143

Roast Jersey Royal salad with maple syrup, confit garlic, red onion & crispy pancetta 42

Roast Jersey Royals with glazed pear, Roquefort cheese & walnut salad 44

Roast pheasant with orange & onion marmalade & juices 120

Roast potatoes with thyme 142

Roast rabbit loin in pancetta with Moroccan-style couscous & calamari 122

Roast rack of pork with baked apples & soft Parmesan polenta 126

Roast red onions in their skins 143

Roast scallops with avocado, French beans & hazelnut dressing 48

Roast venison loin with parsnips, cardamom-scented quinoa & medjool dates 128

Roasted lobster, triple-cooked chips & béarnaise sauce 98

S

SALADS

Carpaccio of fillet with a horseradish bavoire & woodland mushroom salad **32**

Roast Jersey Royal salad with maple syrup, confit garlic, red onion & crispy pancetta **42**

Roast Jersey Royals with glazed pear, Roquefort cheese & walnut salad **44**

Sardines

Gazpacho soup with grilled sardines on toast **68**

Sauces

Béarnaise sauce **204**

Madeira sauce **205**

Tartare sauce **205**

Scallops

Chicken & potato soup with scallops, chorizo & chicken scratching **60**

Curried scallops with coconut & coriander dahl & apple salad **38**

Roast Scallops with Avocado, French Beans & Hazelnut Dressing **48**

Yellow fin tuna with lime & white radish dressing & Bloody Mary jelly **54**

Sea bass

Sea bass en papillote in Asian aromats **100**

Sea bass poached in confit lemon butter with asparagus & Royal Bay oysters **102**

Sea trout

Sea trout with asparagus & pink grapefruit sabayon **104**

SHELLFISH

Cockles cooked in white wine with shallots, pancetta & basil **80**

Curried scallops with coconut & coriander dahl & apple salad **38**

Dressed crab with spring onions, toasted sweetcorn, red chilli & coriander **84**

Fresh oysters with three dressings: cucumber pickle, shallot & red wine vinegar, gin & tonic mint jelly **41**

Linguine with mussels, chorizo, tomato & herb vierge **156**

Lobster salad with marinated fennel & chunky spicy guacamole **90**

Risotto of shellfish **96**

Roast scallops with avocado, French beans & hazelnut dressing **48**

Roasted lobster, triple-cooked chips & béarnaise sauce **98**

Sweetcorn & basil soup with crispy tempura crab claws **74**

Yellow fin tuna with lime & white radish dressing & Bloody Mary jelly **54**

Shoulder of lamb cooked in hay with lavender, herbs & garlic **130**

Slow-cooked belly pork glazed with honey & grain mustard **132**

Slow-cooked lamb shank, spring vegetables & basil broth **136**

Smoked bacon

French toast with smoked bacon, maple syrup & rocket salad **18**

Welsh rarebit with cured bacon **26**

Smoked salmon

Smoked salmon terrine with cucumber salad & soft quail's eggs **50**

Warm potato pancake with smoked salmon & scrambled eggs **24**

Traunch of turbot with a smoked salmon, horseradish & spring pea salad **106**

SOUPS

Chicken & potato soup with scallops, chorizo & chicken scratching **60**

Chilled watercress soup with dressed Asian pear & garden peas **62**

French onion soup with thyme & Beaufort cheese croutes **64**

Gazpacho soup with grilled sardines on toast **68**

Minestrone soup with baby courgettes **70**

My mum's ham hock, split yellow pea & barley soup **72**

Sweetcorn & basil soup with crispy tempura crab claws **74**

Spring onions

Dressed crab with spring onions, toasted sweetcorn, red chilli & coriander **84**

STARTERS

Asparagus, roast red onion & Fort Grey cheese tarts **148**

Carpaccio of fillet with a horseradish bavoire & woodland mushroom salad **32**

Chicken liver parfait with apple & quince purée & warm toasted brioche **34**

Crispy poached duck eggs with griddled asparagus **36**

Curried scallops with coconut & coriander dahl & apple salad **38**

Fresh oysters with three dressings: cucumber pickle, shallot & red wine vinegar, gin & tonic mint jelly **41**

Roast Jersey Royal salad with maple syrup, confit garlic, red onion & crispy pancetta **42**

Roast Jersey Royals with glazed pear, Roquefort cheese & walnut salad **44**

Roast scallops with avocado, French beans & hazelnut dressing **48**

Smoked salmon terrine with cucumber salad & soft quail's eggs 50

Sweet chilli chicken with garlic, lemon & coriander 52

Yellow fin tuna with lime & white radish dressing & Bloody Mary jelly 54

Stock

Chicken stock 207

Fish stock 207

Vegetable stock 207

Sunflower seed bread 200

Sweetcorn

Dressed crab with spring onions, toasted sweetcorn, red chilli & coriander 84

Sweetcorn & basil soup with crispy tempura crab claws 74

Sweet dumplings

Lemon curd & deep-fried vanilla sweet dumplings 182

Sweet pickled duck eggs 209

Tagliatelle

Tagliatelle with crispy anchovies, lemon, garlic, chilli & rocket 160

Taramosalata 206

Tartare sauce 205

Tarts

Asparagus, roast red onion & Fort Grey cheese tarts 148

Baked apple tart 166

Cherry almond tart 170

Glazed lemon tart 176

My treacle tart with raspberries & clotted cream 186

Tempura batter 208

Tender-stem broccoli with garlic 143

The Perfect Sunday Roast 140

Tomato

Linguine with mussels, chorizo, tomato & herb vierge 156

Sun-dried tomato bread 198

Traunch of turbot with a smoked salmon, horseradish & spring pea salad 106

Tuna

Yellow fin tuna with lime & white radish dressing & Bloody Mary jelly 54

Turbot

Traunch of turbot with a smoked salmon, horseradish & spring pea salad 106

Vanilla

Baked vanilla cheesecake with blackberries & mint compote 168

Confit of duck legs with vanilla & spiced kumquat chutney 114

Lemon curd & deep-fried vanilla sweet dumplings 182

Vegetable stock 207

VEGETARIAN

American-style pancakes with honey, Greek yogurt & pecan nuts 14

Apple & cinnamon muffins 16

Asparagus, roast red onion & Fort Grey cheese tarts 148

Cheese soufflé with apple, walnut & pomegranate salad 150

Chilled watercress soup with dressed Asian pear & garden peas 62

Crispy poached duck eggs with griddled asparagus 36

French onion soup with thyme & Beaufort cheese croutes 64

Herb gnocchi with broad beans & Pecorino 152

Minestrone soup with baby courgettes 70

Mushrooms à la grecque 209

Risotto of broad beans, wild garlic & Parmesan 158

Roast Jersey Royals with glazed pear, Roquefort cheese & walnut salad 44

Venison

Roast venison loin with parsnips, cardamom-scented quinoa & medjool dates 128

Vinaigrette 209

Walnut

Cheese soufflé with apple, walnut & pomegranate salad 150

Warm potato pancake with smoked salmon & scrambled eggs 24

Watercress

Chilled watercress soup with dressed Asian pear & garden peas 62

Grilled black pudding with fried hen's eggs, forestière garnish & watercress 22

Welsh rarebit with cured bacon 26

Whiting

Crispy whiting fingers in lemonade batter with minted peas 82

Wild garlic

Risotto of broad beans, wild garlic & Parmesan 158

X

Y

Tuna

Yellow fin tuna with lime & white radish dressing & Bloody Mary jelly 54

Yorkshire pudding with onion gravy 141

THANKS

Many, many thanks to the following people and businesses:

Cheryl Rankin
(for her patience)

Abi Nance (we miss you Abi)

Alastair Christie
Jersey Lavender Farm

Alaistair Jerrom-Smith

Ben Hickingbotham

Bohemia Restaurant

Channel Television

Chris Shelton

Chris Vila

Colin Roche
Jersey Watercress

David Hick Interiors

David Nuth

David Scott
Whato Petit
Beauregard Farm

Don Thompson

Ed Le Gallais

Emma Callery

Jamie Racjan
Fungi Delecti

Judy Egré

Fenella Maddison
Torteval Cheese

Louis Jackson
The Fresh Fish Company

Mae Gabriel

Matt Porteous Photography

Natalie Shelton

Natasha Egré

Paul Le Fondré

Philippa Murphy

Rebecca Hardcastle

The Observatory

The Refinery

William Church
The Jersey Royal Company